SHORT CUTS

INTRODUCTIONS TO FILM STUDIES

OTHER TITLES IN THE SHORT CUTS SERIES

THE HORROR GENRE: FROM BEELZEBUB TO BLAIR WITCH Paul Wells

THE STAR SYSTEM: HOLLYWOOD'S PRODUCTION OF POPULAR IDENTITIES Paul McDonald

SCIENCE FICTION CINEMA: FROM OUTERSPACE TO CYBERSPACE Geoff King and Tanya Krzywinska

EARLY SOVIET CINEMA: INNOVATION, IDEOLOGY AND PROPAGANDA David Gillespie

READING HOLLYWOOD: SPACES AND MEANINGS IN AMERICAN FILM Deborah Thomas

DISASTER MOVIES: THE CINEMA OF CATASTROPHE Stephen Keane

THE WESTERN GENRE: FROM LORDSBURG TO BIG WHISKEY John Saunders

PSYCHOANALYSIS AND CINEMA: THE PLAY OF SHADOWS Vicky Lebeau

COSTUME AND CINEMA: DRESS CODES IN POPULAR FILM Sarah Street

MISE-EN-SCÈNE: FILM STYLE AND INTERPRETATION John Gibbs

NEW CHINESE CINEMA: CHALLENGING REPRESENTATIONS Sheila Cornelius with Ian Haydn Smith

SCENARIO: THE CRAFT OF SCREENWRITING Tudor Gates

WOMEN'S CINEMA: THE CONTESTED SCREEN Alison Butler

BRITISH SOCIAL REALISM: FROM DOCUMENTARY TO BRIT GRIT Samantha Lay

FILM EDITING: THE ART OF THE EXPRESSIVE Valerie Orpen

AVANT-GARDE FILM: FORMS, THEMES AND PASSIONS Michael O'Pray

PRODUCTION DESIGN: ARCHITECTS OF THE SCREEN Jane Barnwell

NEW GERMAN CINEMA: IMAGES OF A GENERATION Julia Knight

EARLY CINEMA: FROM FACTORY GATE TO DREAM FACTORY Simon Popple and Joe Kember

MUSIC IN FILM: SOUNDTRACKS AND SYNERGY Pauline Reay

MELODRAMA: GENRE STYLE SENSIBILITY John Mercer and Martin Shingler

FEMINIST FILM STUDIES: WRITING THE WOMAN INTO CINEMA Janet McCabe

FILM PERFORMANCE: FROM ACHIEVEMENT TO APPRECIATION Andrew Klevan

NEW DIGITAL CINEMA: REINVENTING THE MOVING IMAGE Holly Willis

THE MUSICAL: RACE, GENDER AND PERFORMANCE Susan Smith

TEEN MOVIES: AMERICAN YOUTH ON SCREEN Timothy Shary

FILM NOIR: FROM BERLIN TO SIN CITY Mark Bould

DOCUMENTARY: THE MARGINS OF REALITY Paul Ward

THE NEW HOLLYWOOD: FROM BONNIE AND CLYDE TO STAR WARS Peter Krämer

ITALIAN Neo-realISM: REBUILDING THE CINEMATIC CITY Mark Shiel

WAR CINEMA: HOLLYWOOD ON THE FRONT LINE Guy Westwell

FILM GENRE: FROM ICONOGRAPHY TO IDEOLOGY Barry Keith Grant

ROMANTIC COMEDY: BOY MEETS GIRL MEETS GENRE Tamar Jeffers McDonald

SPECTATORSHIP: THE POWER OF LOOKING ON Michele Aaron

CRIME FILMS: INVESTIGATING THE SCENE Kirsten Moana Thompson

SHAKESPEARE ON FILM: SUCH THINGS THAT DREAMS ARE MADE OF Carolyn Jess-Cooke

THE FRENCH NEW WAVE: A NEW LOOK Naomi Greene

ANIMATION

GENRE AND AUTHORSHIP

PAUL WELLS

WALLFLOWER

LONDON and NEW YORK

A Wallflower Paperback

First published in Great Britain in 2002 by Wallflower Press, reprinted 2007
6 Market Place, London W1W 8AF

www.wallflowerpress.co.uk

A catalogue record for this book is available from the British Library

ISBN 978 1 903364 20 8

Book Design by Rob Bowden Design

Printed in Great Britain by Antony Rowe Ltd, Chippenham, Wiltshire

CONTENTS

LIST OF ILLUSTRATIONS

ACKNOWLEDGEMENTS

As always, it is important to note that any book written by an individual author is always an act of collaboration, and that for every page there is normally someone to thank. My acknowledgements, therefore, run as follows:

Firstly, to my colleagues at the University of Teesside – Simon Popple, Paul Watson, Diane Railton, Siobhan Fenton, Chris Williams, Carol Cooke, Su Reid and Helen Pickering, all of whom, one way or another, and sometimes without knowing it, have contributed to this book. Also, to 'The Train Club' – Diane Nutt, David Wright, Bryan Larkman, Chris Stevens, and Eileen Green – whose convivial support has cheered the journeys home and away.

Secondly, to animators, practitioners and other scholars who have supported me in my championing of animation, and provided help and insight along the way. These include Barry Purves, Ruth Lingford, Caroline Leaf, Bob Godfrey, Ray Harryhausen, Joanna Quinn, Richard Taylor, John Wilson, Eric Fogel, Bill Janczewski, David Williams, and Martin Barker.

Thirdly, I would like once again to thank Yoram Allon and all the staff at Wallflower Press for their patience, support and professionalism.

Inevitably, this book is dedicated to my wife Joanne, for putting up with my relentless 'tippy-tap' in the back bedroom office; my son Freddie, for enjoying *Toy Story* for the forty-fifth time; and especially, for 'Lola-Bola', born as we were going to press. To animate is 'to give life to' – how appropriate that this book is written now.

1 WHAT IS ANIMATION ?

Animation is arguably the most important creative form of the twenty-first century. Animation as an art, an approach, an aesthetic and an application informs many aspects of visual culture, from feature-length films to prime-time sit-coms; from television and web cartoons to display functions on a range of new communications technologies. In short, animation is everywhere. It is the omnipresent pictorial form of the modern era. Like all art forms it has a history, but in its particular case there are many histories which are still being researched and reclaimed. Long dismissed as merely children's entertainment, only in recent years has there been clear recognition of animation as an art; as a form that encompasses more than the American animated cartoon tradition; as a medium of universal expression embraced across the globe.

This short study will concentrate on four aspects of animated film. Firstly, its multiple 'histories'; secondly, the forms and approaches that make up its distinctive vocabulary and its intrinsic 'modernity'; thirdly, its problematic relationship to 'genre'; and finally, its equally complex relationship to 'auteurism'. I will seek to contextualise films that may be unfamiliar to the new reader, but I will also be taking for granted some familiarity with Disney features, prominent recent animation in the 1990s, and the high-profile television presence of cartoon/sit-com animation. Again, these assumptions are made on the proposition that any analysis of the animated form of whatever length can only be a variation of seeking to pour a quart into a pint pot, and it is my intention to provide as much of an introduction to the form here as I can legitimately fit in without misrepresenting its importance and value.

Animation as a form has predominantly been understood as a 'cartoon' medium, and largely defined by the presence and performance of Disney animation from 1928 to the present day. It may be argued, therefore, that all other forms of animation may be addressed through the ways they relate to or differ from the Disney model. Many animation studios across the world have sought to imitate Disney aesthetically, industrially, technologically, and commercially, while others have resisted this approach, viewing it as something which may misrepresent their own engagement with the medium.

It may further be suggested that the American cartoonal tradition, in general, has determined how animation should be viewed. The work of the Fleischer Studio, Warner Bros. and MGM, to name but the most significant, challenged the Disney style and approach, but in doing so arguably created a further 'ghetto' for animation in a particular style of character-driven, anarchic comedy. Although there are many arguments to challenge these perspectives, it is worthwhile noting that many studios worldwide have insisted upon using their own indigenous fine arts traditions, mythologies and cultural imperatives in order to differentiate their own work from what may be regarded as a diluted form of American artistic and cultural imperialism. Chinese animation, for example, is often characterised by calligraphic approaches; Czechoslovakia recalls its long tradition of marionette theatre in its puppet animation; and Russian animators prioritise the cut-out and drawn forms in their work.

Another highly contentious, complex, and contemporary issue is the place of computer generated imagery (CGI) in film-making. The era of the post-photographic film has arrived, and while it is clear that for the animator, the computer is essentially 'another pencil', it is also clear that animation and its aesthetics will be affected by the production enhancements afforded by CGI. Arguably, this has already reached its zenith in PIXAR's *Monsters Inc.* (2001), and the novelty of the technique may have passed (see Wells 2002).

Consequently, it remains important to note that while Europe has retained a tradition of auteurist film-making, also echoed elsewhere in Russia, China, and Japan, the United States has often immersed its animation within a Special Effects tradition, and as an adjunct to live action cinema. In many senses, CGI could once again make the art of the animator invisible, using animation within live-action contexts in a way that makes it indistingushable from its context. All this, after many years in which animators, critics and lobbyists have fought for its elevation, and the recognition that animation operates as a distinctive art-form in its own right.

It can be argued, though, that this view has been implicitly accepted by the film industry in the United States because many more feature length animations are being made, and animation has a high profile on television and on the web. It may be further evidenced by the fact that feature length animations had their own Academy Award category for the first time in 2001. But this may be another 'double-edged sword': while giving animation prominence, it may also make it live-action's poor second relation, once again. Problematically, too, many films now have such a degree of animated effects that it may be difficult to prevent certain ostensibly 'live action' films lobbying for an Animation Oscar. Where, for example, would *Star Wars* (1977) or *Jurassic Park* (1993) be without their post-production animation? Interestingly, however, the Oscar category may also offer independent animators who do work to full-length – Bill Plympton, for example – an opportunity to gain recognition in a way that their films never would in the main category.

The issues which accrue around the American animation industry, like this, have served to operate as a distraction from work conducted elsewhere, and indeed, the prominence of the main studios in the United States has also served as a distraction from different uses of animation in America itself. Historians have reclaimed the pre-Disney pioneering era, and insisted upon the recognition of other more experimental traditions as the true measure of the potential, variety and freedom of animation as a form. In recent years, the success, for example, of Japanese *animé*, and the Oscar-winning triumphs of Briton Nick Park, have challenged the hegemony and implied homogeneity of the American product. There is, of course, a whole range of animation from across the six continents that has consistently challenged this, and is worth noting in this context as the fullest example of the appeal of animation to express personal, socio-cultural and national concerns that bear no relation to the American context at all.

Defining animation

Preston Blair, veteran animator of the 'Dance of the Hours' sequence in Disney's *Fantasia* (1940); director of the 'Barney Bear' shorts at MGM; and most famously, the designer of the dancing girl 'Red' in Tex Avery's *Red Hot Riding Hood* (1943), defines animation as 'the process of drawing and photographing a character – a person, an animal, or an inanimate object – in successive positions to create lifelike movement.' He continues:

> Animation is both art and craft; it is a process in which the cartoonist, illustrator, fine artist, screenwriter, musician, camera operator and motion picture director combine their skills to create a new breed of artist – the animator. (Blair 1994: 6)

Blair's comments provide a useful platform from which to engage with the issues addressed in this discussion. Simultaneously inclusive, comprehensive and yet significantly limited, his definition recognises the centrality of drawing in animation; the idea of animation as a craft-oriented process; the implicit tendency in some forms of animation to ape the codes and conventions of 'realism'; and the multiplicity of creative production roles either played out in a quasi-Fordist industrial hierarchy, or conversely, by one person.[1] While these observations suggest an initial set of frameworks by which to address the animated form, it is equally pertinent to take note of their immediate shortfalls. While drawing self-evidently underpins many approaches in animation, the field is characterised by many other styles and techniques – clay animation; puppet or model animation; the manipulation of objects and materials; sand on glass; cut-out and silhouette animation; computer generated animation and so on – all of which use the graphic and cinematic space in different ways. Although it remains the case that animation is a craft-oriented process, it is important to stress that the impact of new digital technologies has profoundly altered the nature of this process, and while in no way minimising the amount of time required to make an animated film of any significant length, it has challenged the myth of the animator presented in Bob Godfrey's *Do-It-Yourself Cartoon Kit* (1961), where 'it takes eight million separate drawings to make the lady's arm move from there to there' and 'the best part of six years working day and night to complete that particular movement'!

Blair's attention to the idea of creating 'lifelike movement' is also predicated on the assumption that Disney's now orthodox hyper-realist styling, informed by close engagement with authentic, anatomically viable movement forms, is *the* predominant language of animation. Clearly, this need not be the case. More developmental and experimental forms of animation (see Wells 1998) frequently strive for the very opposite effect, where notions of the 'lifelike' are jettisoned and other expressions of

configuration and movement are privileged. Maureen Furniss has suggested that consequently, all animation may be placed within a continuum between *mimesis* and *abstraction*, each film operating in a way that places it along the continuum in relation to the varying applications of its representational forms (Furniss 1998: 6). Finally, perhaps the most important of Blair's perspectives is the recognition of the number of roles that combine in the creation of a certain type of animated film, each in a sense having claim to a mode of 'authorship'. These roles may change and vary, however, within the making of any one animated film, and may even be transfigured in a way that facilitates small groups or individuals to make films, and as a consequence of that process, arguably challenges aspects of the definition of an auteur as it has been predominantly constructed in live-action cinema. This issue is one of the central preoccupations of this book.

Where Blair is completely correct is in his view that 'animation is a vast and virtually unexplored artform' (Blair 1994: 7), and although a great deal of work has been done in recent years to address this, each new exploration is of great value. This particular discussion cannot in itself redress the shortfall, but it will seek to introduce the form and consider ways in which the distinctive vocabulary of animation may be applied to issues of genre and authorship. It is not the intention of this book, however, to reiterate the history of animation, but to draw from its rich and various traditions in order to pursue issues concerning the distinctiveness of animation as a visual language, the particular ways that this distinctive language has been used in order to facilitate an authorial signature, and the inflections upon generic orthodoxies which render genre films in animation as notable sub-genres in their own right. The 'Animation Timeline' provided in the Appendix should be used as an *aide memoire* by which the reader can engage in a range of issues explored in the following pages which may encourage further research.

First though, some further considerations of the 'definition' of animation, or as may already be clear, the self-evident variety of definitions which may enable the widest possible interpretation of the 'openness' of the form. Fundamentally, to make an animated film, it is necessary to create the illusion of movement frame-by-frame through a variety of technical applications. This apparently simple concept, like Blair's perspectives, hides a multitude of possibilities. As Bugs Bunny is the first to point out in Scott McCloud's influential study, *Understanding Comics: The Invisible Art*, animation is more than just 'sequential visual art', provoking McCloud's graphic alter-ego to note that 'animation is sequential in time, but not spatially juxtaposed as comics are ... however, you might say before it's projected, film is just a very, very, very, very, slow comic' (McCloud 1993: 7–8). This observation becomes of interest for two reasons. First, it points up a pertinent relationship between the codes and conventions of comics and animated films, stressing that in the case of animation, images move through time, and that it is the act of *recording* the individual frames which enables the form to move beyond proto-animation – best illustrated by a 'flip-book' in which figures and forms appear to become animated if we 'riffle' consecutive pages – and become 'an animated film'. Second, it draws attention to the individual cels or frames, particularly in the field of two-dimensional cartoon animation, as specific works of fine art made distinctive by virtue of their necessary place within the 25 frames required to make one second of full animated movement onscreen. Significantly, such frames, particularly drawn from the 'Golden Era' of American studio animation now constitute highly collectable art-works in their own right, but arguably, while promoting the aesthetic qualities of a once-neglected popular form, this misrepresents the very specificity of motion at the heart of animated film which is its intrinsic art. Animator Richard Taylor has noted:

> It is more important to emphasise that the quality of the sequence is more important that the quality of the images. It is possible to make a bad film with beautiful drawings or models – the art of the animated film is in the action. (Taylor 1996: 7)

In what has become one of the most oft-quoted insights about the animation process, master animator Norman McLaren suggests: 'How it moves is more important than what moves ... what the animator does on each frame of film is not as important as what he or she does in between' (quoted in Solomon 1987: 11). In his first statement, McLaren directs the animator to think about the act of movement and what it is seeking to express. This is just as relevant to the viewer of animated films in the sense that this very concentration on the specificity of movement is one of the key defining elements of animation, as its creation is of a different order and of a greater freedom than that determined by live-action film. The animator can create 'action' which is outside the vocabulary offered by its mainstream counterpart. The potential reorientation of the physical and material environment under these terms and conditions also re-configures the ways in which the psychological, emotional and physical terrain may be explored and expressed.

Crucial in this is McLaren's second observation. While the material recorded on any one frame of film is unique and fundamental to any animation, McLaren suggests that the animator's creative process, evidenced in the decisions that the animator makes in the continuing application of paint on paper, the manipulation of clay, the 'tweak' of a model and so on, but which occurs *between* the frames, more accurately defines the animator's art. This view creates a major problem for the viewer or critic. Under these conditions the intrinsic nature of the animator's work, like that of the comic strip artist, becomes in McCloud's term 'an invisible art', but once again McCloud's insights about comic design, and the function of the 'gutter' space between individual panels may be of some help here. He suggests that the artist is in essence inviting the reader of images to achieve some degree of 'closure' in reading the information and implication of one image in order to achieve an 'associative' relationship with the following image. This process also shares some characteristics with the concept of montage, but in the case of animation this finds its application on the most detailed and minute scale.[2] The animator must ensure that technical, aesthetic and conceptual continuity is achieved frame-by-frame, and that the 'closure' implied in any one sequence of movement, or in any one tendency in the visual ideas being practically conceived, reveal its associativeness to the viewer in the *flow* of imagery. Again, by tracking the very process by which the smallest constituent elements of the animated film is made, and looking at the ways that 'closure' is implied through the inter-connectedness of the images, viewers can begin to assimilate the distinctive process in animation where aesthetic choices underpin different forms of narrative, and the visual construction of meaning. The following case studies will seek to consolidate some of these initial points.

Un Point, C'est Tout (*A Point, That's All*) (1986)

Claude Rocher's film, *Un Point, C'est Tout* is a mock-philosophic account of the visual orthodoxies of traditional picture making in the Western world, which are exploited and challenged in a fashion which demonstrates and offers an understanding of the graphic freedoms intrinsic to the animated film. Using the simple premise of challenging the predominance of the 'vanishing point' or 'perspective' in picture making, determined by Filippo

Brunellschi (1377–1446), Rocher reveals that 'life is one long optical illusion' and that 'the eye is an unreliable witness', using his film to undermine 'the unshakeable order of geometry'. By collapsing the simple principle that 'the size of an object is inversely proportional to the distance between it and the observer', Rocher shows how an image of a huge tyre in the foreground and a small man, in perspective, in the background, is fundamentally altered by moving the man into the foreground but retaining his height. This is now a small man standing next to a huge tyre and not a man drawn in proportion to it to reveal the distance between the two objects. A 'realistic' perspective immediately becomes a surreal image. Rocher explores the 'flat planes' of the image rather than those created by perspective drawing and iconic illusionism. The sun becomes merely a flat disk; a man steps over a cliff edge but keeps walking across a space which has not got the depth which the drawing implies; a boat and its occupant shift perspective in a storm and what starts out as a man on a boat becomes a seaman catching the same seemingly tiny boat in his own cap. The most persuasive image of this sort is a train which is moving along a track towards the perspective point on the horizon. When the 'lines' which represent the track disappearing into the distance are transmuted into the orthodox illusion of train track *actually* coming to a 'point', then the train inevitably de-rails. The animated graphic form can reveal this idea in a way that challenges the normal conventions of composition and the illusion of realism, simultaneously creating an engaging and amusing image in its own right. Rocher constantly shifts between the visual implications of two dimensionality if the codes and conventions of three-dimensional illusionism are not respected. His approach reveals that space, time, weight and flow can all be reconfigured in animation for distinctive aesthetic effects.

It is pertinent to recall that in order to resolve these visual incongruities, during its pioneering period the Disney studio developed the 'multiplane' camera. Initially, a painted cel was placed on top of a background and one frame was photographed, but often this did not create the illusion of depth required and was limited if different kinds of lighting were needed in different parts of the scene to create a more theatrical effect. As David R. Smith explains:

> Even more importantly, there was a problem in tracking shots, when a character ran toward a background. It was necessary for the artist to draw large series of backgrounds, each background depicting a

> step forward, to create an effect of a change in distance between the character and that background. Also, if the camera simply moved forward toward a single background as, say, the character moving toward a cabin, the cabin would naturally become larger as he approached, but so would the moon painted above the cabin. Audiences were quick to notice these inconsistencies and it did create damage to the illusion of reality that Walt was trying to create. (Smith 1987: 39)

Disney experimented with 'dimensional' effects as early as *Three Orphan Kittens* (1935), but the multi-plane camera itself debuted in *The Old Mill* (1937). Simply, four vertical struts were constructed to accommodate six panes of glass spaced at various intervals with the camera looking down from the top. The pane of glass closest to the camera would have foreground imagery placed or painted upon it, and each succeeding pane would have images in perspective until reaching the final pane, which would have the distant background. Each pane would effectively be a different 'plane' of action, and could move from side to side, and back and forth to facilitate the maximum degree of authentic movement through space. This is particularly effective, for example, when Snow White runs terrified through a wood in *Snow White and the Seven Dwarfs* (1937). Significantly, though, this drive for 'hyper-realism' in Disney films seemed to fundamentally refute the intrinsic vocabulary of the form – that is, the ability to challenge the parameters of live-action illusionism, and the very tenets of 'realism' that this predominantly embraces. As Disney moved towards increasing investment in the notion of 'conviction' (see Wells 1997) and anatomical and environmental authenticity, he created a model of animation which only partially used its graphic potential; a potential exhibited in Rocher's witty exploration of visual premises which refute conventional realist principles as they are practiced in orthodox picture making.

Manipulation (1991)

Daniel Greaves' Oscar-winning film *Manipulation* takes this idea further by making a highly self-reflexive film about the process and practice of animation itself. Set on an animator's table we see the ensuing narrative of a simple pencilled figure on a white sheet of paper. Greaves plays with the construction of the figure's body, drawing attention to the materials; spilled red paint initially filling the figure's nominal head and torso, only to be expelled by the animator's oppressive thumb. The two-dimensional figure then has his limbs threaded with needle and cotton by the animator, who subsequently treats the figure as a three-dimensional puppet, making him dance to a light piano tune. The figure is compressed, extended, and convoluted at the animator's will, but succeeds in producing a penknife to cut his strings, and attempts to escape the paper. The rest of the film explores this relationship further as the animator plays out the cruelest and most violent effects on the figure; he is flicked, stretched, squashed, rolled up, spun, concertina-ed, blown-up and released like a balloon, and humiliatingly 'smudged'. In time-honoured cartoonal fashion the figure survives unharmed, and seemingly immortal. He is very angry, however, and his emotions are depicted as a *metamorphosis** (terms indicated with an asterisk throughout the book are defined in the glossary on page 136) of the figure into an explosion of lines, accompanied by fireworks cracking on the soundtrack. This whole sequence is a testament to the graphic freedoms of the form using all of the space to demonstrate the tension between configuration and abstraction. Simultaneously, the figure has 'human' properties but also exists purely as a graphic phenomenon; he is both a sympathetic character and a set of lines. Interestingly, in either state, these models of illusionism still provoke emotion and symbolise particular forms of relationship and meaning. The viewer feels pity for the figure when his face is mercilessly smudged yet the viewer also enjoys the free play of abstract forms that the figure transmutes into. One final transition involves the character actually becoming a three-dimensional figure made up from the scrunched up paper the animator wishes to throw away. Having slipped off the animator's board and into the bin, it seems as though the character has met his fate, but actually he survives, now ironically subject to the vicissitudes of the three-dimensional environment. Greaves provides a commentary on cartoonal excess, the differences between two- and three-dimensional animation, and the seemingly omnipotent power of the animator to create whatever he wishes.

Such knowingness and self-reflexivity is not new in the history of animation, and arguably, such deconstructive devices may be viewed as the intrinsic but implicit vocabulary of animation *per se*, in the sense that they always operate as a resistance to, and difference from, the principles of live-action film-making. Animation, in many ways, always reflects upon its own construction, but in films like *Manipulation*, and most famously, in Chuck Jones' *Duck Amuck* (1953) (see Thompson 1984; Polan 1985;

Wells 1998), this is made explicit, and calls attention to the animator as a specific kind of 'author'. Donald Crafton notes the concept of 'self-figuration' in films like the Fleischer Brothers' *Out of the Inkwell* series, which features Koko the Clown causing havoc in the Fleischer studio, and includes the presence of the animator (Crafton 1993: 11). This can be literal and direct, but ultimately becomes indirect, and even symbolic, raising interesting questions about the presence and affect of the auteur. Daniel Greaves himself has further explored this through engaging with the difference in planes of action in *Flatworld* (1998) which, as its title suggests, seeks to play out the limits of two-dimensional figures within a three-dimensional world.

Terry Lindvall and Matthew Melton address the centrality of self-reflexiveness in animated film and suggest that this is the key aspect of the 'unpredictable articulations of the cartoon', and discuss how animation facilitates the self-conscious *enunciation* of character as a *phenomenological encounter* (Lindvall & Melton 1994: 49–50). Basically, the very artifice of animation requires that the characters, situations, narratives and designs 'announce themselves' as different kinds of 'phenomena'. This challenges the viewer to both recognise that this is 'animation', and therefore different from live-action film-making, and to invest in engaging with animated phenomena as constructs which may relate directly to the terms and conditions of human experience, but equally may offer more complex mediations on socio-cultural and aesthetic epistomologies. Animation intrinsically interrogates the phenomena it represents and offers new and alternative perspectives and knowledge to its audiences. In creating this level of discourse within and about the very language of animation, animated films recover the idea that such discourses must be created, and beg the question of 'who by?' In reaching this point, the idea of 'the author' is also recovered. As Steve Schneider has suggested, 'animation is probably the ultimate auteurist cinema' (Schneider 1988: 30) because in all of its forms it creates a distinctive relationship between its creator, its aesthetic self-consciousness, and the discourse it provokes. Arguably, every animation suggests its own authorial signature.

Synchromie (1971)

Undoubtedly one of animation's greatest auteurs, Norman McLaren constantly explored the boundaries of animation in a range of works. His authorial signature was, in many senses, this very diversity, as he explored a variety of techniques from painting directly onto film; scratching in film stock; creating chalk-drawn metamorphoses; using Pixillation; animating objects; and manipulating live-action footage (see Russett & Starr 1976).

Synchromie is an abstract film which seeks to create what has long been the desired outcome of many 'Fine Art' animators: the depiction of 'visual music'. McLaren takes this literally, however, by wittily using the 'soundtrack' as it appears on the film itself as the visual aspect of the image. The duration of any one note of the quasi-'boogie-woogie' tune McLaren uses as his electronic soundtrack constitutes the duration of the elongated and sometimes distorted, oblong shape it forms within the *mise-en-scène*. The soundtrack is perpetually present as the dominant visual image within a changing colour scheme, and an increasing complexity of bars, oblongs, blocks and grids are configured in geometric lines, all created by using and re-using the dynamics of the sound as they are literally conceived on the celluloid. This playfulness is the hallmark of McLaren's work, but is merely one aspect of the attention he calls both to the *materiality* of the form, and the *methodology* of its construction. Sound, for example, is an often overlooked aspect of the construction of the animated film, because understandably there is often a preoccupation with the visuals, but the importance of the soundtrack cannot be overstated. From *Steamboat Willie* (1928), the first sound-synchronised animated cartoon, right through to the contemporary era, sound has often been the very stimulus for animated narratives, and a prominent aspect of its distinctiveness. All animated films require a soundtrack to be specifically constructed for them. There is no diegetic sound intrinsic to the recording of the animation itself as there is with live action. All music, vocal performances, sound effects, and acoustic atmospheres must be artificially determined to match the imagery. This may range from voiceover to dialogue to song to instrumental music to electronic noise but the deep suggestiveness intrinsic to sound – itself an abstract phenomenon – is a fundamental part of animation's unique vocabulary. McLaren draws attention to this fact by making sound itself, the imagery of movement and dance.

The Weather (1995)

Scott McCloud has suggested that representational forms in graphic works are essentially characterised by the movement from *photorealist* forms to more *iconic* constructs, which intensify suggested symbolic meaning in minimalist graphic forms, through to *abstract* imagery which effectively abandons orthodox configuration (see McCloud 1993). George Barber's *The Weather* echoes this formulation in the playful engagement with the conventions of the weather broadcast, using the figure of a babbling weatherman interacting with the electronic weather graphics. Barber rejects the 'spectacle' of CGI, rejecting the 'fly-pasts' and perpetual travelling through three-dimensional perspectives and spaces so characteristic of its early uses, preferring instead a more traditional approach which shows the versatility of CGI. The 'photorealist' aspects of a revolving globe give way to the 'iconic' symbols of the weather graphics – clouds, arrows, depression bars and so on – which in turn, bemusingly for the weatherman trying to give his forecast, become 'abstract' colours and forms in globules and tunnels. This simple idea once again foregrounds the associative language imbued in the animated form, and the ways in which the 'technology' works in the service of the art form, and not merely as a recording device. Animators constantly seek to ally traditional techniques with progressive technologies, refreshing and re-inventing the form in a spirit which constantly speaks to the view of animation as a 'modernist' art (see Chapter 3).

Pencil Story (1995)

The success of *Toy Story* (1995) created a 'professional' aesthetic for CGI which, while not creating an 'orthodoxy' for the form nevertheless confirmed the potential of the medium by fully exploiting its distinctive credentials. The toys exemplified the 'plasticity' and 'gloss' of geometric forms created in CGI, while the movement through the domestic space properly revealed the sense of depth and space in virtual three-dimensionality. Disney's *Dinosaur* (2000) takes CGI fully into the realm of hyperrealism, configuring plausible dinosaurs in a real-world environment (see Cotta Vaz 2000), even advancing *Jurassic Park* which, in fact, only had what amounted to six-and-a-half minutes of CGI in it. This scale of achievement with the new digital technologies has all but hidden the animation at its heart, preferring to heighten the sense of realism until the form does not 'announce' itself as animation but insists upon its representational validity. As United Productions of America (UPA) did in the immediate post-war period with their use of *reduced or limited animation** to challenge the aesthetic and socio-cultural orthodoxies of the Disney output, so have independent artists in the CGI era worked to once more 'individualise' CGI environments to distinguish them from their 'professional' aesthetic. Moira Marguin's *Pencil Story* uses child-like drawings, which foreground their simplicity and 'amateurism', as the 2D characters existing in a 3D space. A little girl searches for her black pencil, and having found it, when frightened by her cat when drawing a 3D frame for an imaginary television, hurtles round the room ultimately scribbling and scrawling vehemently on the inside of the screen that the viewer is watching through, thus obscuring the domestic set behind it. In a 3D version of 'taking a line for a walk', the black pencil line exists in space as a graphic idiom in its own right, seemingly taking on material properties and filling the domestic environment. The wonderfully petulant scrawl of frustration and bedevilment that concludes the sequence is at one level a clever recall of the 'pencil' as animation's intrinsic tool, and the pioneering graphic openness in the work of Otto Messmer, the creator of Felix the Cat, while at another level, both an exposé and critique of the smooth, flowing, geometric accuracies of the CGI form in the hands of the major animation companies. Its playfulness is enhanced by a soundtrack which echoes fairground carousel music, and in recalling the pencil, the basic instrument of animation, it also re-signals the presence of the artist, one of animation's most identifiable traits. Equally, Marguin recalls both the intimacy and emotionality of the environment in the figures of the girl, her family and the cat, and resists the mimesis of many 3D environments by engaging with the iconic and abstract values of a primally inspired, 'primitive' context.

This first chapter has been concerned with foregrounding the principle conditions of animation and some of its self-reflexive applications. Having identified the nature and form of animation, the next stage is to evaluate its multiple processes.

2 THE ANIMATION PROCESS

First principles

The process involved in making an animated film is dependent upon the technique involved; the 'studio' undertaking the film; the budgetary constraints and the broadcast context. While the process has common elements in every approach, there are significant differences – for example, in the execution of a 'puppet' or 'model' animation from a 'drawn' or 'cel' animation, or a 'clay' animation from a computer generated film. To a certain extent, the technological factors that underpin the process are also significant in its aesthetic outcome. Self-evidently, three-dimensional approaches are made in a different way from two-dimensional work; the three-dimensional sometimes has more in common with live-action film-making, and its use of 'space' may require a higher degree of conformity with the physical laws of the natural world than, for example, animation exploring the freedoms of the two-dimensional graphic space. Three-dimensional 'clay' animation, however, may have a greater flexibility for the fluid metamorphosis of forms. Puppets made with solid armatures and solid wire or wood infrastructures will obviously have less malleability in this way, but used as the basis for the virtual wire frames within a computer-generated interface may secure the implied solidity and verisimilitude of the figures, while simultaneously providing a more adaptable infrastructure for movement and rendering. These are cursory initial observations concerning sameness and difference in the animation process but immediately it should be clear that in identifying these technical issues that a number of aesthetic, and crucially, authorial issues must be addressed.

The controlling idea

All animated films – like all proposed creative works – start with a concept, a central 'controlling idea' (see McKee 1999: 114–17) that generates the questions which must be answered in order to facilitate the most appropriate way that the idea may be explored in the animated form. The initial idea may be a desire to tell a particular story; the need to address a specific theme or topic; the imperative to test the parameters of art-making for its own sake; the urge to provoke, amuse, hypothesise, make a statement, or insist upon a point of view. The first requirement in engaging with the concept, though, will be at least a provisional decision about *how* it is to be addressed, and what technique will be best suited to its execution and expression. One decision might precede another, or happen simultaneously, but will normally consolidate a mode of narrative and an apposite technological apparatus. As in most film-making practice, a basic story, an extended treatment, and an initial script may be required, but animation – particularly experimental animation – offers the immediate opportunity to reject these processes for more improvisational or less premeditated creative work. The most important question which requires an answer is the simple one of why a film-maker would use animation as the preferred process of work in the first place?

As Jenny Roche has noted, 'the visual challenges of animation are immense', but 'there is no set which is too expensive or exotic; there is no stunt which is too difficult ... the scientific laws of physics, biology and chemistry are no restriction either' (Roche 1999: 137–8). This 'freedom' has its benefits and drawbacks. Simplistically, the more these freedoms are embraced the more distinctively 'cartoonal' or 'avant garde' the animation becomes, while a more conservative exploitation of the possibilities of the form sees a greater alignment with the characteristics of photo-realistic live-action cinema.

Design, visualisation and sources

Most animation, however, begins to facilitate its essential premises when it moves to what may be termed the 'design' stage. This is effectively the visualisation of the proposed idea or story, and normally includes the process of storyboarding – the construction of a sequence of images which begin to give an indication of how the narrative will be expressed in visual terms, and begins to explore the pictorial vocabulary which will prompt the intrinsic 'motion' that is the very imperative of the animated form, however abstract or surreal. The storyboard in effect concentrates on the graphic depiction of developing action, potentially taking into account compositional requirements, possible camera angles and framing issues, and signifying the basic tenets of character design and narrative context.

A specific 'model sheet' will be created for each character which accords with the overall visual styling chosen for the film, which may have a number of previously determined visual reference points. This 'styling' may relate to a particular form of fine art practice – for example, in Frédéric Back's *Crac!* (1980), he particularly emphasises the spontaneity of the line and expressionist shading to capture the energy at the heart of the French-Canadian communities he represents, not merely recalling the fine art influences of Degas and Monet, but the work of local painters Horatio Walker and Cornelius Krieghoff who recorded the landscape of Quebec and the life of its people. Japanese *animé* auteur Hayao Miyazaki, however, reaches back further, to the tradition of 'Garden Art' and the work of the 'Floating World' painters Utamaro and Hokusai, combining this with the aesthetics of modernist Japanese live-action cinema and the hyper-realist effects of 'Golden Era' Disney. British animator Richard Ollive, animator of the Tetley Tea Folk and the Ribena Berries in a number of commercials, also made a small masterpiece with *Night Visitors* (1989) which draws upon a whole tradition of English caricature going back to James Gilray and Thomas Rowlandson, but also takes into its vocabulary the pictorial nuances of Gustav Doré's work and the sleek lines of Aubrey Beardsley. Its main visual source, however, is the children's book illustration of Arthur Rackham, John Tenniel and Richard Doyle. These visual sources do much to enhance the authenticity of the work in playing out the technical dexterity and historically determined meanings underpinning the graphic outcomes (see Chapter 3). Again, these particular modes of styling inevitably support an authorial position that places itself within a tradition in order to draw from it, but also to further enhance it, and 'modernise' its principles. This sense of 'historicisation' in the work offers depth to the artistic endeavour that is evidenced in the creation and treatment of the imagery, while encouraging the appropriation of the 'modern' through animated applications.

FIGURE 1 *Sinking of the Lusitania*

Visual sources may not be merely confined to the traditions of fine art practice and graphic design, of course, and often seek to reference the social and cultural environment in which the narrative of a film may take place. This may be especially pertinent to modes of documentary or propaganda in animation, and include Winsor McCay's *Sinking of the Lusitania* (1918), Disney's *Victory Through Air Power* (1943) and *Our Friend the Atom* (1957) (see M. Langer 1995: 65–97), Jan Svankmajer's *Death of Stalinism in Bohemia* (1990), and Robert Jefferson's Otto Dix-influenced work in Peter Kershaw's *Wilfred* (2000). All these films rely on a full recognition of the time, place and historical circumstance that informs the visualisation process.

Beyond fine art and socio-historical sources, one of the key aspects of visualisation may be the previously established graphic mode created by a particular studio. This is perhaps an aspect most associated with the authorial signature of a major animation studio, and which effectively becomes its 'brand'. The Disney studio may be viewed as the epitome of this visual branding and, arguably, the aesthetic approach defined by the studio in its 'Golden Era' between 1928–41 was predominantly determined by the industrial process which created it. Further, such an industrial process and its aesthetic outcome became the benchmark technically, artistically and commercially, which defined the animation industry *per se*, and has endured and remained influential – for good and ill – into the contemporary era. Although modified by technical innovation, such a process has determined a visual styling in animation, predicated on a 2D cel animated (now digitally enhanced) approach, which in the public imagination and popular culture at large defines the form. Arguably, CGI has changed this to a small extent, and the success of Henry Selick's *Nightmare Before Christmas* (1993) and the Aardman studio's *Chicken Run* (2000) (see Martin 2000) may herald a wave of model animation features, but the Disney 'look' prevails even in the work of Dreamworks SKG's *The Prince of Egypt* (1998) and Fox's *Titan AE* (2000). This raises interesting issues about the 'visualisation' process at Disney, and the need to consistently facilitate a 'known' iconography which defines the 'Classic Disney' style (see Wasko 2001).

The Disney precedent

Robin Allan has addressed what he terms the 'all-pervasive iconographic power' (Allan 1999: xv) of the Disney image, locating its most persuasive effects in the influence of European artists as diverse as Daumier, Doré, Grandville and Busch. Most significantly, though, Allan's analysis of the key works of the 'Golden Era' – *Snow White and the Seven Dwarfs*, *Fantasia* and *Pinocchio* (1940) – returns the reader to consider the implications of the creative process when making an animated film. Allan details the confluence of aesthetic influences and industrial processes in the act of visualising and creating graphic motion pictures – a fundamental element utterly neglected or taken for granted by many textual critics. Ironically, this merely exposes why art-making of this kind within an industrial infrastructure inevitably results in sometimes exemplary and extraordinary outcomes, but equally may result in work of an ambiguous and ill-conceived nature. Clearly, Disney, who Allan interestingly describes as 'a controlling editor' (Allan 1999: 1) – a view of authorship that we shall return to – drove these projects with a passion and a vision; his considerable talent compromised only by his refusal to acknowledge and properly credit the individual contributions of those who serviced his arguably contradictory role as 'moderniser' and 'populist'. One suspects that this is the very tension, both in the man himself and at the studio, that on the one hand could achieve 'art' that can take its place in any history of progressive visual cultures, and on the other, could create material of potentially unsupportable sentiment and cliché. Arguably, there is a direct correlation between the quality of the work and Disney's investment in it; seemingly, the more he withdrew from the animated films and pursued his other preoccupations, most notably his television shows and the creation of his theme park, the more the work becomes dated, unimpressive, and considerably less complex. This view champions Disney as auteur, a concept we will address in Chapter 5, analysing the multiple perspectives from which Disney's role may be understood. Suffice to say at this juncture, however, that Disney's insistence upon the maintenance of a particular aesthetic which defined his studio's practice, also effectively defined the art-form.

Interestingly, although Allan does not mount a consistent and evolving argument about the role European art plays in determining the overall Disney aesthetic, he does note the specificity of the particular visual imperatives which inform the 'process' of image creation in any one Disney text. Such a process, sometimes seemingly arbitrary, can compliment, compromise or enhance Disney's 'storytelling', but equally, while facilitating narrative, the visual styling may compromise the meanings in the text. The *aesthetic* intentions of the Disney artefact, during the time of actually being made, far outweigh any consciousness of its ultimate meaning and cultural effect (see Wells 2001b). The imperative to create entertaining stories which may be executed through an industrial model inevitably means that artistic compromise is necessary. Ironically, the traditional forms of 'fine art' which are the preparatory materials for the film – the extraordinary inspirational paintings, sketches and original designs of the Disney artists – is lost in the translation of these sources into an industrial process that requires simplicity and ease of reproduction.

Visionary work by artists and designers as diverse as Sylvia Holland, Kay Nielsen, Gordon Legg, and Mary Blair regrettably does not find proper purchase on the screen. Stan Spohn's painting of Mickey Mouse, dwarfed in the darkness and gloom of a cave, for example, is of a considerably different quality and tenor than the imagery it inspired in 'The Sorceror's Apprentice' sequence from *Fantasia*. Although the final achievement of the film may remain an aesthetic tour-de-force, the sources and evidence of its process arguably results in the view that fine art is sacrificed to the fundamental requirements of the industrial model. This is one of the reasons why many artists working in the field of animation do not want to work within the major studios as they wish to preserve the distinctiveness of their art in a form which they, as individuals, can use.

In recognising the demonstrable influence of artists like Gustav Tenngren in the Germanic visual style of *Pinocchio*, or the witty ideas of Albert Hurter in the development of an extraordinary range of gothic grotesques or art nouveau contexts in the Disney films, it is possible, however, to foreground the unrecognised talents of those who were defined only in the service of Disney's 'idea'.

This prompts some important questions. Chiefly, how does this reconfigure a view of Disney's 'authorship', and further, how does the commercial and industrial infrastructure of such a studio process compromise as well as facilitate its art-making process?

It is difficult not to conclude that Disney was a great 'producer', and his influence profound, but most importantly was his assimilation of his artists and their work within a practice and an aesthetic orthodoxy which matched his assumptions about his audience's taste. His concern was to prefer design strategies that facilitated what might be termed 'direct' or uncomplicated emotions, *not* artwork which provoked contradictory or complex feelings, and required contemplation. It is in this that Disney saw the radical difference between the effects of painting and the needs of cinema, but in reality, this legitimised an aesthetic that has rarely been able to transcend the limited archetypal meanings associated with particular image forms. It is little wonder that many critics have *only* seen sentiment and domesticity in Disney films because this has become the inherent 'meaning' of their design culture. Arguably, on certain occasions Disney films possess a quality which transcends this aesthetic, and further, still improves upon the performative self-consciousness and melodramatic formulas of live-action film. Most significantly, however, in creating this 'orthodoxy' Disney created a mode of 'visualisation' which the field could aspire to, or challenge.

It is clear that the maintenance of a particular view of 'authorship', and the desire to sustain a consistent studio 'house-style' results in serious issues arising when this perspective is challenged. In *Fantasia,* for example, it was the work of Oscar Fischinger, creator of the influential abstract film *Composition in Blue* (1935), which did not meet Disney's requirements; his own sense of individuality and authorship sitting uneasily with Disney's desire for control; his more abstract use of the medium does survive in the film in diluted form, but is compromised by Disney's aesthetic template. In recent times it is useful to look at the work of Gerald Scarfe, the British satiric caricaturist, in relation to *Hercules* (1997). Scarfe's inspirational drawings for the project demonstrated a spontaneity of line and a brutalist harshness that did not sit easily with the customary *squash 'n' stretch** cuteness of the Disney canon. Further, such design principles set considerable problems for the animators as such body-forms set seemingly insurmountable difficulties in the animation of plausible, anatomically correct, viable movement – even in simple cycles. Complex sequences and routines seemed out of the question. Inevitably, while retaining the overall look and dynamic of Scarfe's designs, Disney's staff modified them to facilitate a house style and to ensure that a hierarchical industrial process could be applied to the visual concept and its anticipated narrative.

This has happened in varying degrees in the production of most animated features made by large studios, where visual and conceptual compromise is a necessary component of the process. With this particular kind of artwork, the visionary intensity and authorial impact of the individual artist is lost to the industrial animation process, surviving at best in the background, and evidenced in diluted form in the standardised graphic idiom of the final film. While this must be frustrating and potentially disappointing for the artist at the individual level, it is a necessary part of a process in which individual contributions are subsumed within a collective enterprise, and issues of authorship remain highly problematic. Richard Dyer, for example, in a useful summation suggests that it is possible to look at 'individual authorship' (either in the way that the director may be attributed with the whole work, or core themes over a number of works); 'multiple authorship' (the work of a whole team in the construction of a film); 'collective authorship' (a specific and consistent working group creating a text) or 'corporate ownership' (the organisation or social structures that produce films) (Dyer 1986: 172–181).

Such issues will be pursued later, but Allan's crucial point stands up, however. He argues that the European cultural influence, embraced by Disney and his artists, is ironically the major factor in what became acknowledged as intrinsically 'American' cartoonal masterworks. He proves this conclusively by demonstrating that the work of the post-war period, which was intrinsically more 'American' because of the self-consciousness about nationhood required during the war, and far more 'fragmentary' in its subject matter, construction and execution, was intrinsically less persuasive and certainly far less the 'Disney' of old (see Allan 1999: 175–204).

A further irony might be suggested in that the Disney films of this period demonstrate a higher degree of experimentation and reference to modern art idioms than at any other time in the studio's history. However, this was something fiercely resisted by Disney. As Marc Eliot notes:

> When Walt returned from Europe and screened [*Toot, Whistle, Plunk and Boom* (1953)], he was appalled at its unrepresentative, non-Disney visual style and lack of formal narrative. Walt and [its director, Ward] Kimball argued vehemently over the film. Frustrated by what he took to be Kimball's obstinacy, Disney at one point considered firing his animator, and would have done so if *Toot* had not won the Academy Award for Short Subject (Cartoon) of 1953. Nevertheless, Walt explicitly banned all further stylistic experimentation by any animator and limited Kimball's participation in future film productions. (Eliot 1994: 218)

Script to sweatbox

In whatever way the visual concept has been explored and extended through the storyboarding, character-modeling, and design process, it remains continually subject to analysis and revision. The decisions made within this pre-production phase are fundamental to the actual execution and assembly of the film. The finalised script, for example, becomes especially significant at this stage in that in actually telling the story, fixing the dialogue, and prioritising the events that constitute the plot, these become the chief descriptors for the further development of character alongside its visual conception; the main basis for the soundtrack (including vocal performances, music and sound effects); and the blueprint for the additional work in the storyboarding enhancement process, signaling the initial conception of movement in sequences and the types of exchange between characters. Roche argues that 'characters need to have an unambiguous, stronger and clearer personality than a live action or even a picture story script, as artists will need to convey a character visually through actions and expressions which can be exaggerated' (Roche 1999: 140). These artists, while they will work with the inspiration of the vocal track and the nuanced performances of the voice actors, nevertheless have to become 'actors' in their own right, and this results in animators having to formulate their own mode of performance practice to facilitate the execution of the acting process through two-dimensional or three-dimensional characters in another form. As Ed Hooks has noted:

> A good animator must go through the similar process of motivating his characters on a moment-to-moment basis, but she must keep re-creating the same moment over and over and over again, sometimes for weeks on end, while she captures it on the page or computer screen. Actors learn that once a moment is gone, it's gone for good, but animators have to pitch camp at the intersections of movement and emotion. (Hooks 2000: 5)

The animator must necessarily predicate the performance on the ways that characters move, and by concentrating on the relationship between action and reaction, facilitate the physical signifiers which illustrate and prompt emotions. This is a process of textual explicitness that must perpetually signal the imperatives and objectives of the characters. I have discussed elsewhere that the animator, in order to achieve this, must not merely engage with an almost Stanislavskian process of identification, but also embrace other performance techniques and theories – most notably in relation to dance – which play out a vocabulary of gestural and muscular signifiers of psychological and emotional response (see Wells 1998: 104–121). By 'embodying' these responses the animator can express them through the materials and aesthetic principles in animation.

Hooks admires the acting processes in Brad Bird's *The Iron Giant* (1999) in which he identifies the clear objectives being pursued by the characters in each scene; empathetic aspects in each character which are based on detailed observation of human behaviour; and modes of conduct which promote a clarity in the expression of character emotions from lust to sympathy to indecisiveness.

Crucially, however, these aspects are bound up in the overall design strategy of setting the story in the midst of 1950s Cold War America, and an ostensibly 'real' environment which prompts neo-realistic performance practices in the characters. This necessitates a mode of authenticity in the design which recalls 1950s American culture, but which also facilitates the fantastical aspects of the story – essentially the presence and impact of the Iron Giant and his relationship to a little boy and a small-town community. This 'reality' is tempered by the way the design moves beyond merely reflecting and recording a historically determined time and place, but facilitates metaphor and mood. This may require a 'colour script' for example, which looks at the colour styling of the narrative across its visual structure throughout the film. Simply, this might identify a light/dark/light/dark visual structure throughout the story which enhances the narrative development and underpinning themes. *The Iron Giant* benefits greatly from such a schemata.

Throughout the whole animation process, however, there remains a constant attention to the material with a view that it may be necessary to revise, change, add, and so on. Tom Hanks indicates, for example, that for his role as Woody, the pull-string cowboy in John Lasseter's *Toy Story 2* (2000), he was involved throughout the whole three years of its production, recording and re-recording vocal tracks as the film was continually evolving.[1] One of the first indicators of a possible revision process is when the 'storyboards' are shot on to film to create a 'story reel', which is sometimes allied to a provisional soundtrack in order to get a sense of the proposed film. It must be stressed that the kind of large-scale process discussed here self-evidently characterises the main production houses, but such a process, however modified or reconfigured, also underpins the much smaller-scale work of independent artists who are seeking to make conventional narrative-based films. Either process is still predicated on the traditional scriptwriter's idiom of 'show, don't tell', which is especially important in animated films. These are intrinsically *visual* pieces, that in many senses should be less reliant on dialogue or voiceover as an expositional imperative. This is why the 'physical' performance of the animated character, or the colour dynamics across the design of different environments and contexts is especially important.

The editorial team, led by the director, and usually composed of the producer, the layout artist, the production designer and the art director, approve the 'story reel' and/or recommend changes and developments, usually addressing the sequences in the film and the particular order in which they should occur. In what is known as the 'workbook' or 'scene planning' stage the actual *mise-en-scène* of the film is addressed, fixing the separate shots and camera moves in relation to the placement of the characters, props and events within a particular scene. 'Rough layout' effectively composes the scene, and suggests how the characters will move through animation, and how the cinematography will work to enhance the action. The 'story reel' is then further enhanced with the beginning of the animation process in which supervising animators create the key drawings which underpin the movement within the scene, and the needs of the frame-by-frame development of the action.

Over the years, there has been a shift from the way some of the early pioneer animators using 'straight-ahead' animation to a near-standardised process of creating a 'pose-to-pose' process, where the key animators established the main poses and other animators 'in-betweened' the movement between them. John Canemaker explains:

> Straight ahead animation is drawn from position A to position Z, one drawing after another. Winsor McCay used a 'split' method. He divided an action into sections – extreme poses – which were filled in with 'in-between' drawings. In this way, McCay knew where his action was going and could control it, which is why his animation is so well timed and contains such strong story-telling/acting poses. Straight-ahead animation is fine for eccentric, funny action, but the control possible with the 'extreme/in-between' method made it the system of choice when sound came to animation in the late 1920s. (Canemaker 1996: 72–3)

It is important to stress that it is the concentration upon movement which is the determining factor of this process, and the first indication of the way that the animation itself will fulfil the needs of the proposed narrative. This is the key difference from live-action film-making. The movement within it is intrinsic to the performances of the actors and the impact of post-production effects. Animation has to rely entirely on the artificial construction of visual performance and events, and is wholly made through the self-conscious appropriation and assimilation of both live-action and fine-art principles by the animators themselves. They are responsible for every aspect of what is necessarily a highly detailed process of *creating* a world rather than merely *inhabiting* one.

The 'sweatbox' is a crucial moment in the development of a film. This is where rough animation scenes in animatic form are viewed in order to see if all the elements work together and to eliminate any errors before the sequence goes to its 'final line' stage. Roger Noake notes that the animatic has considerable advantages over merely working from a storyboard:

> The real timing of the film can be gauged more accurately and adjustments can be made if necessary ... the animatic needs to be read, like a storyboard, as a plan for action, not a substitute for it. (Noake 1988: 35–6)

Obviously, this model of cross-checking occurs in different ways according to the process being adopted in any one production. There are now far more instances of the use of immediate video-playback, particularly in relation to stop-motion animation, in order to look at previous movements and their accuracy. CGI is increasingly flexible in the ways motion can be modified or shapes and forms re-configured and rendered within the computer environment. Under-the-camera film-making cannot work in this way, and many animators make copious notes and sketches to record their impressions of previous and forthcoming frames in the animation. In 'industrial' forms of animation, the 'sweatbox' session may result in radical changes or the recommendation that the work proceeds to 'clean-up'. In other methods, changes may include re-shoots or re-working material, but given the provisional nature of this stage, these tend to be modifications. On *Snow White and the Seven Dwarfs*, however, Disney famously excised two scenes – a bed-making scene and a soup-eating scene – well into their line-test animation stage because he felt that the inclusion of these scenes would slow the pace of the narrative and add little that was already in other scenes. With the sweatbox negotiated, the layout drawings are completed, and enhanced into backgrounds, and character sequences proceed to their 'final line' stage.

Effects to exhibition

Once the animated film has been built in a scene-by-scene fashion into sequences, and these sequences both constitute and consolidate the narrative structure, with their key animation in place allied to a basic soundtrack, work can be done to enhance both the aural and visual effects. The soundtrack is enhanced through an attention to sound effects and music, synchronised with the appropriate imagery to heighten the visual concept, and bring emphasis to the use of dialogue. Visual effects – essentially anything which is not character or object animation within a perspective environment – are added to the scenes, and may be fundamental to the set-piece spectacle that now often characterise full-length animated features. *The Prince of Egypt*, for example, has the extraordinary computer generated 'parting of the Red Sea' effect, but also a whole range of natural phenomena including sand, rain and misty atmospherics. These effects are crucial in heightening the emotional intensity and metaphoric suggestion in the image, and must compliment the background contexts and the character animation which takes place against it.

'Effects' may be perceived in a number of ways. The brief description given here is of a process available to industrial-scale full-length feature animation productions, and a rich tradition and skill in its own right – one, for example, epitomised by Ub Iwerks in his return to the Disney studio following the comparitive failure of his solo career. Animation itself, however, is also often perceived as an 'effect' within live-action film-making, for example in the work of Ray Harryhausen in feature films from *The Beast from 20,000 Fathoms* (1953) to *Clash of the Titans* (1981) in which his stop-motion animated creatures and figures were the central aspect of the narrative and spectacle (see Chapter 5).

Arguably, virtually all contemporary cinema is reliant on animation as the key source of its story-telling devices and effects. As Simon Pummell has remarked regarding *Alien III* (1993): 'It represents cinema teetering between the narrative (will the story be resolved at the end?) of classical cinema and the plastic spectacle (the monster) of digital and special FX cinema; in fact, the cinema of animation' (Pummell 1996: 299). This 'composite' cinema has always sought to make its animation invisible, however, and with it, issues of authorship and questions of 'realism' (see Wells 2001c). These issues will be discussed later, but here it is important to note that an animated film has its own conception of effects, and that even outside the feature film environment, these are also aspects of the independent animator's work in the achievement of specific kinds of imagery and affect. From off-the-shelf software packages for computer generated films through to the specific manipulation of images through a variety of techniques, the animator can determine a 'special' effect which characterises the whole look of a film (for example, in the pioneering efforts by Lillian Schwartz in using computer-abstracted photographs in *Pictures from a Gallery* (1976) or the xeroxing distortions in David Anderson's *Deadsy* (1990)). Animators perceive 'effects' merely as part of their own creative process, however, and not a post-production instrument for live action.

In whatever way the 'effects' are perceived, contextualised and executed, they become part of the totality of the work whether in feature-length or short form, but increasingly, even with independent artists, the films are composited digitally in the computer environment to enhance the levels of assembly and to assist with the checking procedure. This is perceived as the most economic and efficient way of checking for consistency in the combined processes and in the final 'inking and painting' of the complete frame in a pixel-based model. The director and his team continue to work through each aspect of the film, reconciling any issues, checking for continuity, and ensuring the composite is consistent. The

FIGURE 2 *Pleasures of War*

use of the computer should not, however, be thought of as merely the instrument of the big studio. For example, the animator Ruth Lingford, in her films *Death and the Mother* (1996) and *Pleasures of War* (1999), has re-defined the 'plastic' gloss-orientation of much computer-generated imagery by returning to a style which echoes wood-cut engravings, and boldly juxtaposing black against white, or counterpoints an image with a vivid red, in recalling the traditional 'frame', and the graphic illusionism of depth. The computer has enhanced the production process by offering ways in which previously time-consuming tasks can be achieved much more quickly, but even in spite of the considerable achievements of the *Toy Story* films (see Wells 2001b), the innovation of computer generated aesthetics is still in its infancy.

Once the digital composite is transferred to film, the animation is ready for exhibition. The *Toy Story* films heralded a version of animation for the post-photographic era, but animation remains vital and fresh in all its approaches and forms. In whatever technique – computer generated, cel, model, clay, mixed-media, cut-out, drawing on film, under-the-camera manipulation of materials – the processes are comparable but individualised, nuanced by the imposition of generic considerations and authorial intent. Before embarking on how these aspects inform the nature of the process and its outcomes, however, it is necessary to properly define animation as an intrinsically 'modern' art that facilitates 'difference' and 'otherness' in the creative enterprise.

3 ANIMATION : THE MODERNIST ART

In the first chapter it was suggested how animation had a distinctive language of expression, and in the following chapter we examined some of the applied processes used in creating animated forms and some of their implications. It can be argued that historically, aesthetically and technologically, animation is an intrinsically modern form. In all of its incarnations and progressions it has sought to 'modernise' its own process, outcome and cultural import. I have written elsewhere, for example, that the whole history of the animated cartoon in the United States is both a realisation of its own modern art principles, and a social history of modernity (see Wells 2001b). This may be developed further in relation to the whole field of animation, as the development of the form has always embraced the conditions of 'modernity' in a significantly different way than the two acknowledged periods of 'modern' cinema in live-action film, between 1914–25 and 1958–78 (see Orr 1993).

Animation, throughout its history, has necessarily had to embrace the distinctive characteristics of its own vocabulary in order to define itself as an art form in its own right. As well as delineating the form, and determining its intrinsic difference from live-action cinema, in the form of the cartoon, animation emerged in a range of other developmental and experimental techniques: using clay, puppets, sand, objects, materials, paper cut-outs – in fact almost anything. Each new form of animation suggested another 'modernity', aesthetically and socio-culturally progressive. Live-action cinema soon developed its 'classical' model, embracing experimentation limitedly in the form of 'art-cinema', and new technological imperatives largely in the spirit of an 'effects' tradition, or as part of the enhancement of cinema as 'spectacle'. Virtually all forms of animation, however, have been predicated on experimentation in one form or another and certainly have been in the continual embrace of technological progress. One should add that the so-called conditions of the 'post-modern' – reflexivity, parody, inter-textuality, pluralism, bricolage and so on – have always been present in animated cinema, and are the intrinsic aspects of its long-established self-enunciating vocabulary, and the heart of its perpetual modernity, artistically and socio-politically. Even in its most popular forms, animated films constitute an avant garde preoccupied with the conditions of the modern, and its synthesis of art and culture.

Madan Sarup has noted that 'one of the characteristics of the avant garde is the availability to it of and its mastery over artistic techniques of past epochs. It is through the efforts of the avant garde that the succession of techniques and styles has been replaced by a simultaneity of the radically disparate', and with this the prioritisation of surprise, unpredictability, anti-establishment thinking, and an engagement with the 'institution' of art itself (Sarup 1993: 142). Animation has always foregrounded these conditions and interrogated their parameters, seeking to continually expose the complexities of its own illusions, in order to offer the simultaneity of insight and reference. Each image offers a set of associations but equally interrogates the very principle of representation. The 'otherness' of animation itself announces a different model of interpretation which is abstracted from material existence and offers up the transparency of 'ideas', which Susanne Langer notes operate as forms or phenomena:

> They exist only for the sense or the imagination that perceives them – like the *fata morgana*, or the elaborate, improbable structure of events in our dreams. The function of 'semblance' is to give forms a new embodiment in purely qualitative, unreal instances, setting them free from their normal embodiment in real things so that they may be recognised in their own right, and freely conceived and composed in the interest of the artist's ultimate aim – significance or logical expression. (S. Langer 1973: 50)

This is the fundamental principle of the self-enunciating vocabulary of animation, and the self-figuration (see Chapter 5) which underpins the mode of authorship in animated forms. Further, it is the condition by which the fleeting and ephemeral may find concrete expression, and comment upon transcience and change. Animation in essence makes the aesthetic surface of the work more visible, tracking the implications of motion, and offers a perception of spectacle as well as its outcome. This creation of what might be viewed as a 'virtual' space simultaneously signifies the mediation of aesthetic principles, but equally provides a context where the very principles of lived experience psychologically, emotionally and physically may be revealed as the intrinsic vocabulary of socio-cultural existence. As Langer again suggests, in regard to the work of fine artists:

> Nothing demonstrates more clearly the symbolic import of virtual forms than the constant references one finds, in the speech and writings of artists, to the 'life' of objects in a picture (chairs and tables quite as much as creatures), and to the picture plane itself as an 'animated' surface. The life in art is a 'life' of forms, or even of space itself. (S. Langer 1973: 79)

It is this principle that is literally enacted in animated film, and consequently prompts, at one extreme, the quasi-photo-realism or hyperrealism in the depiction of the 'life' of forms, or at the other, the completely abstract exploration of planes, surfaces, and materials. This enables the animator to simultaneously embrace the 'modernity' of progressive art-making, while also interrogating the 'modernity' underpinning social progress and development.

The following points seek to define and illustrate the ways in which animators work in relation to ways that fine art practices are translated into the principles of animation and further, how this constitutes an avant garde approach, even within populist forms, that continually re-determines the conditions of the 'modern' while representing aspects of 'modernity'. Fine art principles (draftsmanship, model-making, painting and so forth) are central to the animation process, but while these modes of expression are crucial in defining the animated aesthetic, they are not ends in themselves. The translation of these practices into approaches to animated film, however, reveals the process of the practice itself, as one of the unique aspects of the distinctive vocabulary of animation.

One of the key challenges for fine artists working in traditional aesthetic media, implied in Langer's statement earlier, is to suggest the illusion of movement through static forms. Animation enables the fine artist to reconcile this issue by using the film medium to show how the movement they wish to suggest is actually enacted. Walt Disney, in his 1950s television series, began his programme 'The Art of the Animated Drawing' by including ancient examples of art-making which sought to show movement : the cave paintings of six- or eight-legged animals seemingly in motion at Lascaux; the comic strip-like sequence of people in motion in Egyptian hieroglyphics; and Leonardo da Vinci's anatomical studies. Disney immediately demonstrates the pertinence of animation by showing these images in motion. Images like those painted on a cave wall or engraved in stone, the epitome of art made for eternity, advance their qualities in the contemporary era by virtue of being made to move. The animals run; the Egyptians move from one 'extreme' posture through to another 'extreme' posture in a fight sequence, moving through the various static positions of the struggling figures that determine the motion of the conflict; the da Vinci figure comically moves his legs from side to side. These animated sequences actually illustrate the motion implied in the image, and simultaneously, draw attention to the process of making animation.

As a development of this outcome, animators seek to use established techniques from fine art practices to create similar aesthetic outcomes in motion. These approaches are often informed by a recourse to the classical or 'Masters' tradition in order to simultaneously authenticate the inspirational sources used, the qualities imbued in the animation itself, and acknowledge the modernity of the animated form in enhancing established forms. Oscar Grillo's *Rembrandt* (1992) uses the master's late paintings, for example, as the visual catalyst to explore Rembrandt's own recognition of the aging process and the inevitability of death. More importantly, Grillo uses the 'illuminated' quality which is central to Rembrandt's aesthetic as a metaphor. A flame is extinguished implying the dying of the light, and an empty canvas further highlights the onset of death. Grillo captures the very meaning of light in Rembrandt's work but through animation adds a layer of meaning which not merely signals the importance of this luminescence within the paintings themselves, but an insight into the artist. Yuri Norstein takes this one stage further in *Tale of Tales* (1979), where Rembrandt's luminous aesthetic is self-evident, in which he explores the potent qualities of memory, dream and lucid consciousness as moments of illumination, aesthetically and psychologically. Norstein suggests that our recollections and unconscious – our way of thinking – is intrinsically pictorial, and that the heightened states we experience are captured with a particular emphasis; an emphasis that he captures in his work through the intensity of a Rembrandt-like use of colour, form, light and atmosphere. In this case,

Norstein uses the 'plasticity' and 'malleability' of Rembrandt's style to foreground the use of animation as an apt recorder of the emotive internal human condition (see Wells 1998: 93–7).

Such was the potency and affect of the cartoon tradition in the United States, particularly in the work of the Disney studios, in creating a dominant visual aesthetic for animated film, other animators working in different ways and in different cultures and traditions sought to maintain their own aesthetic distinctiveness by playing out fine art practices within their own local, regional, and national contexts as models of significant and oppositional indigenous work. This merely reinforced the Disney model as the 'orthodox' currency of the animated film, and all other models as a 'developmental' aspect of this approach, or an 'experimental' approach which was overtly different (see Wells 1998; Furniss 1998). Arguably, the Disney aesthetic makes the fine art conditions of its construction invisible, while all other methods essentially privilege the sense of their process, and its inherent relationship to fine art as their creative endeavour.

We have already mentioned the ways that Fréderic Back and Hayao Miyazaki use their own national traditions to inform their work, but one of the most pronounced cases is the work of the Wan brothers at the Shanghai studios in China where, in 1936, having acknowledged the major influence of the Fleischer brothers on their work, they argued for a more indigenous cinema, and insisted upon the recognition of Russian and German animation as of equal quality to the American output (see Quiquemelle 1991). *The River is Red with Blood* (1938) followed. Based on a traditional poem by Yue Fei, a Song dynasty general, and with a chorus sung by the Wuhan chorus, the film, concerned with the Sino-Japanese conflict, takes on the style of contemporaneous Chinese graphics and recalls the traditional statues sometimes associated with Shang-period burial rituals. *Songs of the Anti-Japanese War* (1938) retains a graphic style that not merely insists upon its Chinese pictorial ancestry as a resistance to American forms, but also to any Japanese styling which may be ideologically charged. Effectively, in the field of animation, the fine art traditions of indigenous cultures are translated into moving iconographic statements about art and ideology in their specific contexts.

Animators re-interpret established stylings in relation to the ways that this imagery echoes and facilitates an approach in animation. For example, Jean-François Languionie's *Crossing the Atlantic By Rowing Boat* (1978) uses a cut-out styling which directly echoes Georges Seurat's 'Sunday Afternoon on the Island of the Grand Jette' (1885–86), thus drawing attention to the

FIGURE 3 *Crossing the Atlantic By Rowing Boat*

contrived composition of vertical and horizontal lines in the objects and shapes used, as a signal of an 'impressionistic' dreamlike quality of the perception of the events. Languionie's work also recalls Henri Rousseau's 'The Sleeping Gypsy' (1897) in using a child-like approach to compositional orthodoxy which offers associations with a more primal or innocent engagement with imagery.

To return to Fréderic Back, the particular influences and their effects on the meanings of his films may be traced in his embrace of Edgar Dégas' 'The Dancing Class' (1874) with its use of unconventional viewpoints, asymmetry and the illusion of 'spontaneity'; Claude Monet's 'Springtime' (1874), which employs the visual effects of light and movement to determine an 'objective' record of landscape; and Paul Cézanne's 'Montagne Saint Victoire' (1886–88), which gives a sense of the apparent transience of the durable, and the need to interpret nature's discourse through colour. Richard Williams' title sequence and interpretive interludes throughout *Charge of the Light Brigade* (1963), however, seek to embrace indigenous sources of caricature and political satire to counterpoint Charles Woods' highly ambivalent respect for, yet scepticism about, military expertise and endeavour. This leads him to echo James Gilray's 'Fatigues of the Campaign in Flanders' (1793), a critique of the pleasures and spoils of war, and Charles Williams' 'The British Atlas' (1816), featuring John Bull literally supporting the 'peace establishment', commenting upon the drive for defence cuts in the light of a 150,000-strong standing army. The animators in each case reveal the inherent aesthetic and ideological meaning of their pictorial forbears by making implied movement meaningful through its literal execution.

Animators self-consciously recognise that fine art practices and modern art principles are intrinsically related, and constantly evolving and progressing. This is sometimes depicted literally and metaphorically in the language available in animation. The evolution of a form, for example, can be shown through metamorphosis, while a progressive social or political agenda can be expressed through a new technique or approach. This both reflects the 'openness' of the vocabulary available in animation, and seeks to ally form and meaning in the text. In Sheila Graber's *Heidi's Horse* (1987), the evolution of a child's graphic interpretation of a horse is demonstrated through the year-on-year use of her original drawings; Joan Gratz's film *Mona Lisa Descending A Staircase* (1992) literally illustrates the history of art through the metamorphoses of some 35 art styles using 'clay painting' – that is, using clay as a 'painting' material. Gratz notes: 'The main advantage of clay painting is its fluid look. It has some affinities with other forms of animation that are done directly under the camera. Clay painting can create complex colour and give you the texture of brush strokes ... to communicate the emotional content of the works' (quoted in Frierson 1994: 26–7).

Animation can significantly condense time and alter material space, rapidly illustrating change and development. This is especially persuasive in clay animation as the physical properties of the material environment are seen to be in flux, and the principles of metamorphosis more obviously revealed, as the clay literally changes its shape and form in becoming something else. This is particularly affecting in Will Vinton's *Legacy* (1979) and *Creation* (1981), which show huge time periods in the Earth's development truncated into a short form, but offers a coherent view of the consequences and implications of the passage of time, and the impact of humankind upon the Earth. The palpable nature of the 'clay', and its close relationship to the very materiality of the Earth itself readily reinforces the ideas being explored.

Animators, drawing upon a fine art background, not merely explore approaches and stylings, but also self-consciously explore theoretical principles and ideas generated within fine art, and play them out afresh using the animated form. This has already been noted in the ways that animators use expressionist, impressionist, cubist, and surrealist approaches and so on, but becomes more specific in films like Raoul Servais' *Night Butterflies* (1996), which explores the contradiction between the mobility and sound orientation of the animated form and the surrealist work of painter Paul Delvaux, whose subjects are essentially silence and stasis. Using an art deco design, figures move with an almost robotic, animatic quality, their movements having the quality of surreal automata, occupying the same empty bourgeois space explored by Luis Bunuel in live-action surrealism. Lesley Keen's *Taking a Line for a Walk* (1995) engages with Paul Klee's dictum, and literally enacts the possibilities using the single line in the visual determination of characters, contexts, and narratives within a two-dimensional space. Film-makers like Norman McLaren regularly used a theoretical hypothesis as the principle of limitation and exploration in their animation. This usually provoked the use of a new technique or approach, but was always in the service of testing the parameters of a specific idea within the 'open' vocabulary of animation.

Raoul Servais recognised that a key aspect of the vocabulary of animation is the interrogation of the interface between stasis and immobility in fine art, and the free forms of motion in animation. This creates a context for a number of art-practices, but, as has been noted, is particularly revealing in creating new forms of 'surrealism'. The Fleischer Brothers' early cartoons were characterised by innumerable aspects of the *mise-en-scène* moving for their own sake, having their own 'business' which was not necessarily narratively motivated, and at best pointed to a visual joke predicated on the literalness of a 'funny' moving character or object. This fundamentally undermined the coherence of the 'realist' premises which the Disney aesthetic was increasingly moving towards in order to sustain extended narratives in the traditional Hollywood style. Virtually all animated forms may be seen as 'surreal' in the sense that many deliberately juxtapose unusual and unexpected aspects within nominally plausible, authentic and fictionally consistent environments. These incongruous elements can be used for comic purposes, or set up a more challenging mode of visualisation that may possess the quality of disquiet or nightmare. This is both the main currency of cartoonal humour but also of texts which seek to emulate the instability and foreboding of the dream-state or paranoid consciousness.

This mode of 'incongruity' is often used as a method by which animators critique, parody or revise previous forms of art, or indeed, animated practices, re-determining their potential meanings and effects. Marv Newland's

FIGURE 4 *Monty Python's Flying Circus*

Godzilla Meets Bambi (1969) does this with persuasive economy when Godzilla's foot crushes Disney's Bambi, or in virtually the whole canon of Terry Gilliam's work on the 'Monty Python' series where he deliberately undermines the 'classical' status of art works, and re-imbues them with contemporary meanings (see Wells 1997: 60–5). This does not merely occur within ostensibly adult material, but also in relation to the ways that animation studios foreground the particularity of their art. Klasky Csupo's 'Rugrats' series, for example, in episodes entitled 'Art Fair' and 'The Art Museum', play out the relationship between modern art, animation and the child, aligning the children's free-form of expression with Jackson Pollock's 'Action Painting', and interestingly, in their visit to the 'Museum of Feaux Arts', encouraging the children by suggesting that looking at art-works 'helps to broaden children's multi-cultural perspectives by teaching them to see themselves in the art'. Chuckie's potty-training is literally recalled in the seated figure of Rodin's 'The Thinker' (1880), while his more painful experiences are re-lived in their encapsulation in Edvard Munch's 'The Scream' (1883). This is more than referential playfulness, however, as the animation itself seeks to reveal the relationship of the children's perception and emotion as it is mediated through the 'abstractness' of the art. Consequently, the animation reveals itself to be a credible mediator of the relationship between perception (how something is seen), interpretation (how something is understood) and creativity (how something is re-engaged with as the material of expression). This is the essence of the vocabulary available in animation, which simultaneously reveals these aspects as the currency of its modernising potential.

In summary then, the translation of avant-garde experimental practices in fine art into forms of motion both signifies the modernity of the animated form, and arguably, results in the purest from of authorially determined aesthetic practice in animation (see Chapter 5). Animation often reveals its fine art sources by demonstrating the subtextual meaning and process-oriented development of particular art-making, foregrounding its intrinsic modernity.

Further, animators perceive particular approaches to the representation of movement in fine art as determining some of the underpinning principles of the distinctive capabilities of animation. Sergei Eisenstein describes this as 'plasmaticness': 'A rejection of once-and-forever allotted form, freedom from ossification, the ability to dynamically assume any form' (quoted in Leyda 1988: 21). This is especially important in relation to the representation of the body, and may be evidenced in sources as diverse as John Tenniel's caricatures for Lewis Carroll's 'Alice' (1865), Walter Trier's illustrations, Toyohiro and Bushen's early nineteenth-century woodcuts and Hokasai's paintings from Japan, and Wilhelm Busch's glutinous figures 'Max and Moritz', which all find parallels in Ub Iwerks' 'rope' designs for his characters in the early Disney 'Silly Symphonies'. The mutability of the body, and indeed, the whole material environment, is a fundamental aspect of the way animation revises and questions aesthetic norms and social orthodoxies. It is, therefore, a key enunciative aspect in the modernising process as it literally and metaphorically illustrates instability, change and alternative perspectives.

Animators, therefore, embrace specific pictorial traditions which are defining aspects of visual culture as a 'form', and embrace such socio-politically determined images as a determinant of 'meaning'. This self-conscious approach to moving-image making both 'modernises' aesthetics and uses aesthetics to interrogate the conditions of 'modernity'. Consequently, animators reveal popular art forms as fine art practices through their translation into the 'modernity' of animation. This principle is then further circulated in new art works and cultural contexts such as advertisements and paintings. This is most obviously evidenced in the art works which, for example, take up one of the most significant iconographic images of the twentieth century: Mickey Mouse. For example, Andy Warhol's 'Mickey Mouse' (1981), Mick Haggerty's 'Mickey-Mondrian' (1978) and Bob

Buccella's 'Vincent Van Gogh's to Disneyland' (1987) (see Yoe & Morra-Yoe 1991) In these instances, animation re-facilitates and modernises Fine Art itself. As a last point on this it is worthwhile making a brief comparison between Gianluigi Toccafondo's *The Tango* (1991) and Disney's *Tarzan* (1999). Toccafondo explores the ambiguous area between painting and film by using the materiality and impreciseness of 'paint' to move from the figurative to the abstract in *The Tango*, literally moving from the dancing figures of Fred Astaire and Ginger Rogers to a series of animals to a number of pure shapes and forms. Toccafondo essentially investigates the two dimensionality of each image, a separate painting in its own right, and creates a series of paintings for his film which change the nature of the 'canvas' to a recognition of the 'frame'. The changing figures represent the movement from a quasi-photo realism to complete abstraction, revealing the relationship between photography and painting in a way that only animation can readily facilitate. Disney's *Tarzan* takes this a stage further, by using a computer generated 'deep canvas' technique in which the animators can literally create a three-dimensional painting of the landscape, which Tarzan then swings through. This 'deep canvas' technique is a recognition of the ways in which new technologies have re-determined 'perspective' as a moving entity in the frame and enabled fine artists to embrace a 'painterly' response to it. These approaches represent a perpetual 'modernity' in the form which engage with its inherent qualities and antecedents.

In the next two chapters, we will address how this 'modern art' principle underpins the distinctive aspects of animation's embrace of, and differentiation from, 'genre' and 'authorship' as it has been predominantly defined within live-action cinema.

4 GENRE IN ANIMATION

> Basically, genre studies asks two questions: 'What does it mean to say that a film is a musical, western or horror film?' and 'How can we explain the fact that while the topics available to film-makers are virtually limitless, the same types (genres) of films are made over and over again without, it seems, exhausting audience interest in them?' (Allen & Gomery 1985: 85)

'Genre' is at once one of the seemingly most accessible aspects of film form, yet also subject to increasing degrees of debate with regard to its definition and purpose. At one level it is still easy to recognise a 'Horror' film, a 'Western', a 'Musical' and so on, but such is the hybridity of generic elements in many films that there are many aspects of crossover and combination within established genres that in effect, new 'sub-genres' have been created. These intersections and adaptations means that any genre rarely operates in an exclusive way.

Attempts to categorise film genres sometimes work with a high degree of generality, and consequently close inspection often renders categorisation of particular films deficient and contradictory. The immediate question arises as to whether there can be any 'pure' definition of genre in the first place, and if any change in the nature of what might be regarded as generic orthodoxies subverts these genres, enhances them, or undermines them, and to what enduring effect. There is a high degree of circularity in the answer. It is more useful to think of the ways in which particular narrative structures or values work within genres, or in the case we are addressing, within animation as a *form*. What this reveals is that within self-evident genres like Romance, Horror, War et cetera, are generic plots like the *maturation* plot (the coming of age, rites-of-passage story); the *redemption* plot (the transition of the main character from bad to good); the *punitive* plot (the main, ostensibly good character behaves badly and is punished); the *testing* plot (the willpower versus temptation story); the *education* plot (the main character moves from a negative perception of the world to a more positive outlook) and the *disillusionment* plot (the reverse process, from a positive outlook to a disenchanted one) (see McKee 1999: 79–99). This approach is enabling in the sense that it offers a way of looking at genre beyond the determinants of its *mise-en-scène* or typical narratives, themes and so forth, and beyond the institutional or economic conditions of production, and seeks what may be termed 'deep structure'. Having explored the relationship between animation and dominant genre motifs, in this chapter we will define the deep generic structures in the animated form.

Genres emerged with the development of film form itself, but inevitably drew upon previous sources in other media and arts contexts to establish typical visual and aural codings that defined particular kinds of film in a quasi-branded form, both for aesthetic and commercial purposes. Inevitably, certain stories had common aspects in different genres; certain narrative devices were also shared; and specific core themes and emotive scenarios breached implied parameters. This ensured that 'genres' retained a reactionary identity but were often radically progressed, and that all types of audience, however configured, would embrace the generic elements they most enjoyed or engaged with, even in relation to films that ostensibly they might not have immediately empathised with. Stereotypically, this might be illustrated by the view that women enjoyed the 'romance' elements of male-oriented stories about conflict and confrontation in War films. Contemporary audiences are well versed in genre conventions, and effectively work with the films they view, identifying the familiar elements, but also recognising the ways that they have been developed and enhanced.

Realistically, while 'genre' operates as a useful means by which to categorise film, it is often the case that it is re-determined not by the self-conscious repositioning of generic norms, but by the re-working of standard plot devices, and the production trends that follow the commercial success of a particular story that has done this. Again, this emerges out of an attention to 'deep structure', although in these cases this has become explicit. Sequels, for example, are often a re-telling of the same story in the first film, and it is often the case that the first film has drawn significantly upon others. It is not a far step to formula film-making and franchising. The *Scream* series, for example, parodied itself, pastiching the 'stalk 'n' slash' movies like *Halloween* (1978) and *Friday the 13th* (1980), and spawned further 'self-conscious' teen horror films on the basis of constantly re-visiting, repeating but partially revising generic codes and conventions. Any 'fright' that emerged was entirely about the formulaic practices of such movies, and not about any notion of 'fear' relating to real-life experience or real-world activities. The spectators for these films operate as a 'pre-sold' audience – a commercially viable certainty – on the basis of their complete familiarity with the generic 'play' which is central to the films' story-telling engine. This is risk-free novelty which merely adjusts 'likeness' for minimally different ends (see Wells 2000).

Genre is recognised by audiences, theorised by academics, and actually defined by screenwriters and directors working within a production system. All three constituencies share the same understanding of the basic frameworks of the concept. For the purposes of this discussion it is worthwhile to identify some of the ways that genre has been determined, in advance of our discussion of the distinctive genre issues allied to the field of animation.

A genre may be understood in the following ways:

- as a discrete 'category' or 'type' of film which is defined by its visual, technical, thematic or subject-oriented consistencies.
- as a set of codes and conventions, which determine particular expectations and outcomes in the narrative and the *mise-en-scène* of a film.
- as a term predominantly based on the recognition of particular kinds of visual and aural *iconography*, which serve as the key signifiers of an implied common language shared by the makers of the film and the audience, which in turn defines the cinematic construction of the text.
- as a means by which to recognise the ways in which limited and predictable features in the film shape and determine the coherence of a form, and play out a mode of control in film-making practice which ensures typical outcomes and imaginative resolutions to narratives unobtainable in 'lived' experience.
- as an *infrastructure* to film narrative which operates as a mode of order and integration, and may be recognised as the determining

factor which maintains core stories and myths, and ideological stability at the heart of film practice.

- as a system which is subject to change and modification in relation to shifting historical and socio-cultural forces and practices. Each 'genre', therefore, also has its own history and development, often demonstrating the movement from 'innovation' to consolidation as a 'classical' model; progression through 'formal' intervention; and re-definition through self-reflexive or intertextual revision.
- as a framework which simultaneously invites complicity with traditional models, but encourages re-definition through pastiche, exaggeration, intertextual play, re-configured signifiers and so on.
- as a model of *bricolage* in which varying cultural resources are mobilised to 'authenticate' or 'challenge' generic expectations or outcomes.
- as a method by which to obtain some distinctive co-ordinates to define a particular film within a category, which in turn offers the possibility of defining a film as a 'non-genre' text, and potentially, another kind of cinema practice.
- as a *canon* of work demonstrating high degrees of variation in the interrogation of the textual, industrial, commercial, critical and socio-cultural definition of the concept of 'genre'.
- as a challenge to the ways in which *auteur* cinema has been constructed, privileging the generic determinants of the film text itself, over the idea of the personal 'vision' of the director in mobilising them.
- as a set of cinematic conventions largely determined by men, which have absented or misrepresented the artistic, representational and critical aspects of women making film, taking part in film, or theorising film practice. This has led to a number of 'corrective' strategies to address these issues by women film-makers, stars and critics.

Unsurprisingly, these perspectives on genre are predicated on live-action cinema and inevitably, while there is some correspondence in the field of animation, it is clear that animated films pose particular questions of these generic definitions by virtue of their intrinsic difference as a form and as a mode of production which enunciates its own process. Arguably, if animation *is* significantly different from live-action cinema, it may support and relate to established definitions of genre, but will ultimately be defined by its own generic terms and conditions. It is this issue that we shall explore in this chapter, drawing upon the defining concepts included above, but also in suggesting the ways in which animation transcends these paradigms and insists upon models of its own. Robert McKee, for example, has suggested that animation is governed by 'the law of universal metamorphism', and although animation leans towards action genres or farce, and the 'maturation' plot in recent Disney features, in essence 'anything can become something else ... there are no restraints' (McKee 1999: 85). This, of course, creates as many problems as it might immediately resolve in attempting to be more specific about the ways animation interfaces with genre.

Stuart Kaminsky has suggested that genre is essentially 'a body, group, or category of similar works, this similarity being defined as a sharing of a sufficient number of motifs that we can identify works that properly fall within a particular kind or style of film' (Kaminsky 1985: 9), adding some important qualifying terms, 'theme' (a conceptual or intellectual premise), 'motif' (a dominant recurring idea), and 'archetype' (a historically determined symbolic cultural commonality) as underpinning related principles. Within this framework, it is a comparatively simple task to identify animated films within broad generic conventions. For example:

Western	*Dangerous Dan McFoo* (1939)
	Sioux Me (1939)
	Old Glory (1939)
	Western Daze (1941)
	Bugs Bunny Rides Again (1948)
	Texas Tom (1950)
	Song of the Prairie (1953)
	Cowboys (1990)
Horror	*The Story of a Mosquito* (1912)
	The Mad Doctor (1933)
	Dr Jeckyl and Mr Mouse (1946)
	Tell Tale Heart (1953)
	The Metamorphosis of Mr Samsa (1977)
	Harpya (1978)
	Monster City (1987)
	The Sandman (1990)
	Grizzly Tales for Gruesome Kids (2001)

Science Fiction	*Superman* (1941)
	House of Tomorrow (1949)
	The Playful Robot (1956)
	The Jetsons (1962)
	The Victor (1985)
	Akira (1988)
	Abductees (1994)
	Ghost in the Shell (1995)
	Titan AE (2000)

The films identified here all share common characteristics with established generic conventions. For example, the Western films include the iconography of the cowboy and/or Indian, saloon settings, gunfights, implied aspects of frontier history and so on. As in any analysis of a 'genre' film, however, what becomes important is the treatment of this iconography, and in this particular case, the ways in which the particularities of animation interface with the generic expectations and orthodoxies. *Bugs Bunny Rides Again*, for example, plays out the gunfight scenario between Yosemite Sam – 'the roughest, toughest, he-man hombre that's ever crossed the Rio Grande – and I don't mean Mahatma Gandhi' (a line later re-dubbed because of its potentially insensitive representation of Gandhi, and racist connotations in relation to 'Indians', both from Asia and North America) – and Bugs Bunny. Bugs relates himself to Western star Gary Cooper, and responds to Sam's Western cliché assertion that 'this town ain't big enough for the both of us', by rapidly constructing a modern city panorama. It is in this sequence that the cartoon foregrounds its own conditions, enabling the literal interpretation of a phrase in visual terms that could have only been achieved in animation. Sam's 'six shooter' is topped with a 'seven shooter', and ultimately with a 'pea shooter', and the whole concept of the gunfight has been revised in relation to cartoon conventions; so far, in fact, that the cartoon incorporates one of the form's own clichés, by having Sam fall from a cliff. This 'gag' is refreshed, however, by a conscience-stricken Bugs providing a mattress for Sam's fall, only to pull it away at the last minute. A horseback chase is followed by a card game, 'like the western pictures', and a victorious Bugs boards the 'Miami Special' train, filled with bathing belles, ending the cartoon in as incongruous a manner as its parodic treatment makes inevitable. Here the cartoonal form has 'hollowed out' generic conventions to insert comic meanings germane to the animated form, celebrating its own conditions, rather than potentially offering a critique of the genre.

Such a critique partially occurs in Phil Mulloy's *Cowboys* series, featuring *That's Nothing* (1990), which uses bold, brutalist black graphics to depict cowboys in a range of ever-escalating violent sexual acts, equating the male erection to the gun, and defining cowboy masculinity as the pursuit of gratification through conflict. The film ends ironically by parodying the Western cliché of the deep bonding between a cowboy and his horse by having a cowboy copulate with one to their mutual satisfaction and relief. Self-evidently, Mulloy uses the cowboy genre to address the relationship between 'maleness', selfishness and violence, but more importantly, uses the graphic particularities of animation to stretch the visual boundaries that cannot be legally depicted in mainstream film-making. Animation still foregrounds its own artifice, and so enables animators to create imagery that would be largely unacceptable in orthodox live-action contexts. Once more, generic convention has been 'hollowed out' but for much more subversive purposes. Mulloy's work also reflects a different national and cultural position. Made in Britain, the film has a more conceptual purpose which interrogates the assumptions of the generic norms, and takes them to their logical extremes. Different cultural inflections can result in a re-working of the genre which suggests more about the culture in which it is produced, and the makers of the film, than the genre itself.

Globetrotting George Pal left Budapest to make animated advertisements in Holland before arriving in America to make the celebrated *Puppetoons*. His film *Western Daze* was intended as a tribute to the Western genre and American culture, and succeeds in being so until its climax, when the villains, having been chased across the Prairie, fall down a rock face, and a sign appears saying 'There ain't nobody lower than we'. This is partly a self-reflexive joke which echoes the self-consciousness of the Warner Bros. cartoons Pal admired, but while the sign works as a visual pun on the fact that it is literally so, its moral implication sits uneasily with the amoral slapstick universe of the American cartoon Pal had used his puppets to depict up until then. Once again, however, the discourse about the film becomes a discourse about animation rather than an engagement with the tenets of the Western.

It is in this that it is possible to first delineate the distinctiveness of animation within genre debates. While animation may correspond to many of the defining principles cited above, it might be most usefully viewed 'as a method by which to obtain some distinctive co-ordinates to define a particular film within a category, which in turn offers the possibility of defining a film as a 'non-genre' text, and potentially, another kind of cinema practice'. Simultaneously, animation can offer a commentary upon genre 'iconography', 'infrastructure', 'bricolage', 'codes and conventions' and so forth, but also work as an interrogative tool with which to privilege 'difference' and foreground the distinctive credentials of animated forms. This might be seen most specifically with some examples from the 'Horror' genre above.[1] *The Metamorphosis of Mr Samsa*, referred to later in the auteurist section on Caroline Leaf, signals in its title one of the distinctive aspects in animation which enables narratives to work on a different set of principles. People, objects and environments can literally metamorphose from one state to another. The transitions and transmutations which are a staple of horror texts may be literally conceived; moreover, the stories themselves may undergo more fluid transitions which illustrate more persuasively the often surreal terrain which supernatural, extraterrestrial, or subaltern horror stories inhabit. Leaf's adaptation of Kafka's 'The Metamorphosis' also embraces another of the facilitating processes intrinsic to animation. Her condensation of the story is achieved by ensuring that the maximum of suggestion and associative relationship is drawn from the minimum of imagery, and it is in this approach that the importance of the iconographic aspects of generic texts becomes apparent. Sometimes, the most specific of generic signifiers may be all that is required to inflect a particular narrative into a set of infrastructural associations that enrich the capacity of the text. The close-up depiction of Winsor McCay's vampiric mosquito in *The Story of the Mosquito*, for example, is enough to draw the film into a consideration of its place as a 'horror' film. Similarly, Raoul Servais' film *Harpya* uses the generic figure of a harpy to invoke a gothic surreality, but in many senses the film is a sustained joke about consumption.

Where animation is particularly adept at foregrounding its specificity as a form in relation to the horror genre is in the ways that it adapts gothic literature. Poe's 'The Tell-Tale Heart' is effectively a 'psychological' horror story, and the UPA studio recognised that it would have to achieve two things in adapting the story: firstly, to find the appropriate graphic style to present the narrative, and secondly, and inherently related to the first process, to alter the perception of the American 'cartoonal' idiom from its condition as an intrinsically comic space. Disney's *The Mad Doctor* and MGM's Tom and Jerry cartoon, *Dr Jeckyl and Mr Mouse* modified the gothic context in order to explore the relationship between horror and humour, playing out 'suspense' and 'surprise' to amuse rather than frighten. Ironically, *The Mad Doctor* still ran foul of the British censors for being too frightening for children. UPA wanted to achieve a different effect. Consequently, director Ted Parmalee replaces the highly narrativised soundtrack of traditional cartoon with voiceover, the interior monologue of an insane yet regretful murderer, played by English actor James Mason; and uses Dalì-esque modernist imagery instead of comic caricaturial art-work. Parmalee effectively changes the visual characteristics of the orthodox cartoon – highly 'elastic' graphic forms and modes of representation which depict speed and mobility – to an uncertain, less comprehensible space which may be likened to the fragmentation and fluidity of nightmare. Animation is especially persuasive in depicting such states of consciousness – memory, fantasy, dream, and so on – because it can easily resist the conventions of the material world and the 'realist' representation that characterises live-action cinema.

Interestingly, this capability is highly enabling because it can illustrate both states of consciousness and visual conceptualisations of psychological and emotional conditions. *The Tell-Tale Heart* effectively visualises fear, anxiety, guilt and the process of mental decline. Such is the 'openness' of the vocabulary of animation that visual concepts which seek to embrace thought or emotion can be constructed contextually in order to achieve the degree of effect. For example, in *Mr Peeler's Butterflies* (2001), one of Simon and Sarah Bor's *Grizzly Tales for Gruesome Kids*, a children's animated series, the animation is used *implicitly* to suggest that the butterflies that circulate in a child's bedroom are, in fact, the eye-lids that Mr Peeler has cut off as punishment for those children who cannot or will not go to sleep. Conversely, the animation in the Japanese animé *Monster City* is used *explicitly* to exaggerate the grotesque and violent imagery in one of the parallel demon worlds which are common in the Japanese horror genre. In the first example, animation dilutes the possible effect because of its intrinsic artifice, thus making it acceptable within a children's format, while in the second example animation amplifies the possible effect in order to move beyond the conventions of orthodox horror texts. Arguably, the reverse is true, too. Subversive imagery occurs in a space nominally marked out for a children's audience in *Mr Peeler's Butterflies*, while representations of excessive violence in full-length feature films like *Monster City* may be made more acceptable by virtue of the fact that it is merely ink and paint. This is effectively an unregulated space which signals an inherent challenge to live-action representation, and further facilitates flights of imagination which can challenge the narrative, thematic and visual orthodoxies of genre.

The science fiction genre is particularly interesting in this respect. It is a genre which is based on extrapolation, speculation and innovation, and arguably, the genre which most embraces special effects as the currency of its authentic depiction of imagined worlds. Long before Christopher Reeve featured in *Superman* (1978), and the promotion insisted 'You'll Believe a Man Can Fly', the Fleischer Brothers' hyper-realist *Superman* series made during World War Two had already achieved this feat, reconciling Clark Kent's mythical powers with the need for effective propaganda. Superman's powers were the unassailable powers of the United States. Here purposive animation transcends its status as 'a cartoon', and indeed, as a text which is merely offering 'an effect' – a man flying – as its intrinsic spectacle.

Animation has inherent spectacle in the freedom of its graphic vocabulary, but it is a spectacle that has been naturalised into its vocabulary in a way that enables the form to infiltrate generic conventions almost unnoticed. Psychoanalyst Martin Grotjahn has argued that World War Two and its aftermath, the Atomic age, created a culture in which technology could only be interpreted in a spirit of humankind's penchant for self-destruction and annihilation, rather than in a way that stimulated a more creative and productive 'symbol producing unconscious', concluding, however, that this was still at large in the art of the cartoon. He particularly identifies 'some symbolic creations of little men trying to deal with the big troubles of our time ... in Ferdinand the Bull with his passivity, Mickey Mouse with his conquest of the machine, and Superman with his dreams of glory' (Grotjahn 1957: 205–22). The animated form supports the omnipotence of the characters it represents – they do not have human emotional frailties, psychological vulnerabilities and physical ailments; they are 'of themselves' even when having an extensive human referent. Grotjahn's essential point is that the animated figure works as a 'symbol' that transcends materiality, but makes material impact. Crucially, and ironically, the suggestions and suppositions of animated science fiction have a greater degree of authenticity through their presence in a form which does not premise anything which can refute or deny the propositions. This degree of 'clarity' divorced from actuality means that generic orthodoxies can be reflexively addressed, but not necessarily made obvious, ironic or cogent in a way that has become a necessity in live-action cinema.

The Japanese animé features *Akira* and *Ghost in the Shell*, for example, benefit from their unconditional commitment to the naturalised scenarios they are presenting. *Akira*'s post-apocalyptic world refuses any interrogative approach which is grounded in the material world, and consequently it sustains its own system of philosophic enquiry. Its animated form refuses or complicates generic norms *and* factual determinacy, but nevertheless sustains an authentic account of its own perspectives. *Ghost in the Shell*, too, privileges a complex address of the disappearance or illusion of identity in human forms, and its theme of the post-human status is given credibility by the non-objective, non-linear credence of the animated form. Perhaps this is best illustrated by noting Paul Vester's short film, *Abductees*, which animates the recollections by people, sometimes under hypnosis, of their claims to alien abduction (see Wells 1997). Vester uses animation to authenticate the non-referential material of subjective accounts, using the associative, symbolic and illustrative function of the form to validate the claims. He effectively subverts 'documentary' by using the visual tropes of science fiction, but revises those generic hybridities by advancing the inherent artifice of animation as the most trustworthy process in verifying the narratives. Like the animé features, the film presents its own system, part-engaging with, part-refusing the idea of genre 'as an *infrastructure* to film narrative which operates as a mode of order and integration, [which] may be recognised as the determining factor [that] maintains core stories and myths, and ideological stability at the heart of film practice'. Arguably, animation *only* re-invents genre, or dispenses with its intrinsic principles altogether.

Before exploring this possibility further, we will engage with some approaches which have sought to address 'genre' as a structural principle, and in relation to some suggestions about broad 'categorisations' within the animated film. Norman Kagan suggests, for example, that each genre is characterised by a dominant controlling idea: the western as defined through the concept of 'the individual moves community towards civilisation'; the horror film as 'complicity with the abhorrent'; the 'show business' sub-genre of the musical involving 'the compulsion to "perform" and its consequences' (Kagan 1982: i–ii). This controlling idea is played out in three ways: the tragic/heroic; the melodramatic/moralising; and the comic/ironic. These structural imperatives – effectively aligning the super-objective of the generic narrative to the mode of interpretation – localises the particular inflections of genre identification. The tragic/heroic mode principally deals with the relationship between the intense motivation of the central protagonist to succeed in the face of the seemingly insuperable forces of nature, history and culture: a heroic fight that inevitably ends in tragic circumstances. The melodramatic/moralising mode harnesses emotional spectacle to a moral dilemma, and usually an archetypal struggle which defines the parameters of personal and social conduct. The comic/ironic mode parodies genre conventions, subverting their serious intent by inverting, undermining or exaggerating their conditions. Inevitably, among animated films, there are examples which find correspondence to these trajectories. For example, the Greek myths have provided a useful source for animators to play out different generic perspectives.

Barry Purves' *Achilles* (1995), for example, works in the tragic/heroic mode of the original myth, and uses the stylistic tropes of Greek theatre and Aristotelian unities to focus upon the tragic flaw informing the central character that dooms him to his fate. Achilles' flaw is the agency of male romantic desire and homo-erotic bonding in the sexually charged atmosphere of masculine conflict and ambition. Achilles' private needs and yearnings for his cousin Patroclus undermine his public persona and distract him from his engagement with affecting social forces. Purves' achievement lies in drawing upon the chief thematic tendencies determined by Aeschylus, Sophocles and Euripedes, the three key Greek playwrights in the evolution of the tragic form, which effectively become its generic structural imperatives. Aeschylus establishes the conditions of the inevitable fall of the hero, and the ethical context in which this takes place; Sophocles refines this by suggesting that it is the imperfection and aspiration of the hero which causes his downfall, and not the mere tides of fate; while Euripides goes further, and locates the pathological imperatives which frustrate the hero, and are intrinsically related to the contemporary conditions of existence, as the key aspects of decline, rather than the exigencies of history. Achilles' forbidden passion for Patroclus is played out in the midst of the mission to win back Helen from her capture by Paris, whose sexual encounters are bawdily parodied by Achilles and Patroclus in a mock passion play, and heartily enjoyed as part of the heterosexual orthodoxies of military culture. Helen is held at Troy, which is protected by Hector, Troilus and Aeneas, however, and Achilles' task is near insurmountable. The spoils of war amount to the casual rape of captured Trojan women. Achilles' disinterest in the rape of a slave, Briseis, sees him mocked and misunderstood by his men, who measure their commander's status as a soldier by his (hetero)sexual appetites. King

Agamemnon abuses the girl and immediately gains the approval of the men, but Achilles is lost to their cause. Purves sophisticatedly makes the heart of his dilemma his obsessional love for Patroclus, and not his pride over Agamemnon's assertion of his kingship and sexual prowess. The story becomes a tragedy because Achilles cannot reconcile the needs of his sexuality in the light of his warrior creed, and is further compounded when the ill-equipped Patroclus dons Achilles' armour to trick the Trojans, but is murdered by Hector. Achilles takes his revenge on Hector, and wins back his armour – actually his father's – but is himself felled by Paris's arrow in his heel. Purves uses the generic elements of Greek drama to create the culture of Aeschylus; a Sophoclean hero, and a Euripidean modernity which enables him to talk about the complexities and alienation of contemporary gay culture through the epic passions of the enduring myths.

Ray Harryhausen's work in *Jason and the Argonauts* (1963), however, is of a different order (see following chapter). The film is played out in the melodramatic/moralising mode, and rather than adhering to the tragic/heroic mode of the myth, simply accepts Jason's quest as the storytelling engine of the film, and does not play out a personal interpretation of the narrative in the way that Purves does. Rather, Harryhausen's interest is in depicting the fantastical elements and encounters that characterise Jason's journey to recover the golden fleece. Jason's imperative is unquestioningly viewed as a just and worthy cause, and his role merely befits the classical 'Hollywood' hero rather than classical myth. Unlike Achilles, Jason is not represented as a flawed hero, or configured in any way which renders him anxious, doubtful or prone to the vicissitudes of his own hubris. Jason is intrinsically 'right'; his heroism defined by his bravery and ingenuity in the face of gods and monsters. Unlike Purves, Harryhausen wishes to use spectacle as a physical rite of passage rather than a psychological or emotional one. Where Achilles must suffer in order to try and redeem himself, Jason must merely overcome the crashing rocks, the harpies, Talos, the bronze warrior – significantly altered in scale and impact from the original myth – and most memorably, the six sword-wielding skeletons, 'the children of the Hydra's teeth'. These animated sequences are the melodramatic peaks of the film and each battle won sustains the assumed moral order, and the heroic hierarchy of Jason and his crew, which features Hercules. The physicality of the male figures is about strength, endurance and power; it remains unaligned to issues of sex and sexuality. Rather it becomes part of the material culture of the film. If Purves' animated environment is wholly configured through the theatrical staging of three-dimensional puppetry, Harryhausen's animated sequences also serve to stage both puppets and live-action figures as if they were part of a similar theatricality in the *mise-en-scène* of the film. Harryhausen's 'Dynamation' technique requires that live-action shooting takes place, which he then scales his models into and re-animates frame by frame. His essential theme thus becomes the reconciliation of human and non-human forms in a fantasy context. In order to sustain the plausibility of such genres – fantasy, horror, science fiction – these effects must not merely authenticate themselves but sustain the broad moral archetypes and melodramatic imperatives of the narrative. Jason's heroism is legitimised by his triumph over the unknown and the supernatural; Harryhausen's work enables the story to embrace generic orthodoxies and extend them.

Disney's witty television series 'Hercules' (1998) extends the comic parameters of the full-length feature, but uses the Greek myths in a sustained comic/ironic mode. Effectively all the myths are evacuated of their tragic/heroic intensity; removed from any plausible notions of emotionally driven melodrama and archetypal sites of moral antagonism, and used extensively as loose infrastructures for American High School stories and teen preoccupations. 'Who put the glad in gladiator?' is the first line of the signature tune; from 'zero to hero' the story imperative of the gawky Hercules as he studies to be a hero in training under the guidance of Philoctetes, or 'Phil' for short. Mythic characters are reduced from epic scale to everyday dupes; their characteristics and capacities are vehicles for ironic asides. Characters effectively become ciphers for contemporary joke-making. Hercules himself is a sustained joke about the unsupportability of 'heroism' and its accidental achievement; the all-seeing Cassandra is a hip-sceptic, who suggests that Hercules should 'do the math, Archimides' in order to see the obvious; Pericles is a Reagan-like leader who only speaks in folksy aphorisms; Hades, king of the underworld, is a Scorsesian New York hood; while Midas becomes caught up in a James Bond parody. 'Hercules' is intrinsically post-modern in its knowing reconfiguration of the *received* knowledge about the Greek myths. The basic narratives and the dominant aspects of the featured characters in the myths which have passed into the public domain have been used as the core generic referents to create incongruous gags which, in the style of 'The Flintstones', imposes the idioms and currencies of the modern world on its ancient context. All three examples use animation to facilitate similar approaches to genre that are available to live action, however, and differ only in the way that the specificities of animation facilitate particular kinds of storytelling. Consequently, while operating in a similar way to the generic orthodoxies described earlier, this does not significantly comment upon the ways in which animation offers distinctive approaches to genre beyond conventional definitions, except in the way it enunciates its own difference as a form. In many ways the animation enables the viewer to learn more about the mode of interpretation, rather than what is specifically achieved in animation. Arguably, however, in facilitating a method by which 'genre' may be freely interrogated, the viewer is offered an explicit determination of the distinctiveness of animation as a form. If the language of animation becomes clear through this process, the next step is to address whether this language creates any specific genres of its own. It is this aspect of animation that remains relatively unexplored.

Norman Klein, for example, identifies the 'Depression Melodrama', the 'Chase' cartoon, 'the Screwball Noir' (see Klein 1993) as generic examples without locating them in any wider schemata, though it is clear that these definitions may be understood within genre definitions recognisable as production processes in mainstream film. To get closer to definitions of 'genre' in animation, it is necessary to negate this relationship and search for new terms. Richard Taylor has attempted to look at this issue by seeking to place animated films in six distinct categories, although these are inconsistent in the sense that they are part thematic and part contextual. He suggests that animated films may be defined as either *dramatic*, *lyrical*, *didactic*, or *comic*, and as *commercials*, or *children's entertainment*. This is helpful in that it offers a partial stepping-stone towards a closer analysis of animated genres, although the definitions which underpin each category are often brief and general. The 'dramatic' genre, for example, is defined as the 'use of animation to give dramatic strength' (Taylor 1996: 106), and largely applies to films that aspire to dramatic seriousness like *Achilles* above, Ruth Lingford's *Pleasures of War* (see Wells 2001a), or Halas and Batchelor's adaptation of George Orwell's *Animal Farm* (1954), of which Bruno Edera remarks:

> The narration and dialogue had to be fairly limited to have maximum effect, so the animal noises and the music had a very important role in building on the difference and similarity between human and animal sounds in varying moods and situations, and sometimes in conveying Orwell's political asides. There is therefore in

> the film both a dramatic story evolving from the conflict of the characters and an element of continual comment on its meaning. Yet because of its basically serious theme – which can be summarised in the phrase 'power corrupts' – the subtle presentation nevertheless gives the effect of severe simplicity. The result is a unique film which draws its strength from the tension between the lifelike, sometimes comic, interplay of the animals and the simple but tragic idea behind it. (Edera 1977: 128)

Simply, in order to enhance the 'seriousness' of this animation, considerable attention needed to be paid not merely to the nature of the adaptation of a political satire, but in the revision of the cartoon as a vehicle for 'animal' stories. Animals have a central place in cartoon films, and arguably, before *Animal Farm*, their function had largely been comic or comforting, or symbolic at best. The representation of animals also in some ways reconciles the problems of representing 'adult' behaviour in animated human beings, especially in relation to sex and violence, and in response to the advocacy groups who opposed it in cinema *per se*. As Richard Schickel notes, for example, of Disney films:

> Disney, when he borrowed the balletic movements and timing of the silent comics but changed the actors from human to animal form in his cartoons and removed the sexual references from the great routines, effectively disposed of many of their objections. What had been nasty as a form of human behaviour became acceptably adorable as obviously fictive animal behavior. (Schickel 1986: 95)

Halas and Batchelor had to bring a maturity to the animal characters and their presentation if the serious intent of the novel was to be properly embraced in the film. The reconciliation of the difficulty in creating a non-comic cartoon, 'mature' characters in the guise of animals, and a satire with clear political implications makes *Animal Farm* an important 'dramatic' success.

Taylor's second category, the 'lyrical', is defined as 'where the intention has not been to tell a connected narrative [where] the impression [is] produced partly from the high quality of the image, but mostly for the poetic force given to the images by the entire concept' (Taylor 1996: 116). This is largely the area of highly personal, auteurist film-making (see next chapter) and embraces a whole range of films, perhaps those most notably emerging from student contexts and independent artists and production companies. Alison Hempstock's *Growing* (1994) is an impressive example of the 'lyrical' in that it creates a self-contained world which is concerned with a man tending his allotment, growing and harvesting his crops. There is no ostensible story or event, and in essence little 'subject', but the central conceit of the approach – the consistent use of close-up – has the effect of making the representation of common forms and objects abstract and unusual. Further, this creates the effect of a safe, enclosed, womb-like world which pulsates with rich, saturated colours, textures and shapes. Everyday fruits and vegetables are depicted as they grow and enlarge; their bulbous, organic presence wholly tactile and sometimes provocatively sensual. This intense observation of taken-for-granted minutiae in the natural environment re-invigorates both the plants and the manual labour of the gardener, and the effect of the animation which captures the essence of 'life' as it moves through the living things. Animation has essentially invested and enhanced the mundane by foregrounding its purpose and effect, through the use of impressionistic imagery which becomes 'poetic' by virtue of Hempstock's aesthetic application.

While Taylor's definition of the 'lyrical' is readily illustrated by *Growing*, it is clear, however, that similar auteurist films, which may have the same non-linear, almost non-objective quality, may not have a 'lyrical' outcome in the same way. Karen Kelly's *Stressed* (1994), an impressionistic metamorphosis of urban angst, part Otto Dix, part Gerald Scarfe, but ultimately an extraordinary graphic flux involving multiple storylines where individuals confront the frustrations and disappointments of their highly routined and oppressive existences, resists any 'lyrical' outcome which may be viewed as romantic. While there are lyrical elements – a sensual Persian cat, doves in flight, a fire-eater, a stallion – these are the elevated aspects of a brutalist design which reflects the anger and complexity of contemporary personal and social aspiration. The term 'lyrical' in some senses misrepresents the challenging nature of this kind of visual poetry, but equally it recognises its fine art sensibility and source in working through a particular concept that is the central premise of a film, which may be uniquely executed through animation.

Taylor's third category, the 'didactic', simply categorises specific animations with the 'aim to carry a message' (Taylor 1996: 126). This includes Taylor's own notable films for the Larkins Studio and his public information films from the 1970s. The *Charley* series featured a small boy and Charley, his cat, engaged in scenarios that addressed a range of child-centred health and safety issues – the dangers of, for example, playing with matches, near rivers, around cookers, and talking to strangers. The Central Office of Information (COI) insisted that the films must not present the dangers in any way that made them seem attractive. Taylor recognised that the child viewer could be engaged by exploring the relationship between a child and his pet. Children are interested in ensuring that their pets do not come to any harm, their love for their pet prompting a recognition of what constitutes responsible behaviour and safe conduct. Each film, therefore, subjects the cat to the hazard in each case in order that the little boy may reconcile the situation and articulate a clear warning about the dangers his cat experiences or anticipates. This is the message of the film, and while 'didactic', it is not authoritarian, and more likely to be successful in the sense that children can see the consequences of dangerous situations, and the harm they may do, but in a self-evidently artificial way. Intrinsic to this approach is its aesthetic. Taylor suggests: 'I've always felt about animation that the eye sees shapes in patches of colour; the copying nature of defined lines is limiting; animation needs to break out, so I use light and shade as the presiding style.'[2]

The *Charley* films have a simple graphic line which echoes children's drawings but emphasises the nature of the relationships, the dangers portrayed, and the consequences with clarity and poignancy. The visual directness of the style echoes the concept explored. The scenarios set up a 'recipe for disaster' in order that order can be restored by sensible instruction. Charley – speaking through his owner, the little boy – effectively speaks as a peer not a parent, but he speaks as much through his graphic representation as he does his voice (incidentally played by Taylor's daughter, Catherine), because this is intrinsically related to the illustrative mode of children's books and of child-like pictorial exploration. The situations – large configured around 'play' – are also empathetic, innocent in their expression, but clear in their warnings. Taylor brought similar clarity to the far more sobering *Protect and Survive* films he made for the COI in 1975. A Campaign for Nuclear Disarmament supporter, Taylor was invested in the project, and even though he knew there was a high degree of futility in providing this information in the face of nuclear war, nevertheless believed that some information was better than none. The films were politically sensitive and made in a low-key fashion, and remained untransmitted. Each film – *Action After Warnings* (1975) and *Casualties* (1975), a mixture of basic graphics, reduced animation, model work and live action – offers instruction in the event of nuclear attack; its chilling symbols are in retrospect a seemingly naïve distanciation from the real outcomes of such circumstances. By abstracting disorder and death into animated forms, the film suggests a logical and enabling response to inevitable catastrophe.

In many senses, it is this 'abstraction' that is afforded by animation that enables 'didactic' films to embrace, on the one hand, exaggerated forms of propaganda, while on the other offering clarity to educational principles and ideas. In *Bugs Bunny Nips the Nips* (1944), Bugs can give the Japanese ice-creams containing grenades; in *Weather-Beaten Melody* (1942), a gramophone and a suspender strap left abandoned in a field are hints of subversion and decadent resistance to an oppressive Nazi regime; while in *Songs of the Anti-Japanese War* the 'pen' of the Chinese 'intellect' can overcome the brutality of the Samurai 'sword'.

The Leeds Animation Workshop have specialised in making a range of films about social issues, often underpinned by feminist agendas. *Through the Glass Ceiling* (1995), created by Jane Bradshaw, Milena Dragic, Janis Goodman, Stephanie Munro and Terry Wragg, co-opts and contemporises a range of fairytales to explore discrimination and inequality for women in the workplace, wittily pointing up the sexism and lack of economic common sense in male-dominated business practices. The animation is used to literally depict the 'gender salary gap', the 'typing pool' and angelic 'high flyers', each commenting upon their status as 'jargon' and heightening the reality of their implications. This works as agit-prop, raising political issues and provoking debate in an informed, astute and clear way, once more using the counterpointing innocence of the animated form to engage with serious models of social enquiry. Numerous school programmes have included animation for teaching and learning; *El Nombre* (1999), for example, dealing with simple maths problems in the setting of a sub-spaghetti western. Disney specialised in such films during the 1950s with a series of instructional animations on health and safety matters made for 'The Mickey Mouse Club' television series. Hosted by Jiminy Cricket – Pinocchio's 'conscience' figure – shorts like *I'm No Fool in Water* (1957) advise about swimming, while *You – The Living Machine* (1958) demonstrates the inner workings of the human body. The 'didactic' form of animation best illustrates what I have termed elsewhere 'penetration' (Wells 1998: 122–7), because it uses animation to visualise processes which would be both invisible, unimaginable and potentially incomprehensible. Effectively, the animation 'penetrates' into the areas which cannot be conceptualised and illustrated in any other form.

Taylor's category of the 'comic' – films 'primarily to provoke laughter' (Taylor 1996: 150) accommodates virtually the whole cartoon tradition and its derivatives; and the further contexts he offers which especially embrace the animated form, 'commercials' and 'children's entertainment', are informed by animation which uses the four approaches defined above. Taylor's perspective on commercials is useful, however, in the sense that he notes that this is animation made to 'a specific brief for content and length' (Taylor 1996: 132) but whose large budgets and need for immediate visual distinctiveness paradoxically enables a high degree of experimentation and the development of new techniques. From Oscar Fischinger's abstract marching cigarettes in 'Murati Marches On' (1934) to Craig Zerouni's three-dimensional Walking Man for Canon Photocopiers to Richard Purdum's 'Smart-i-llusions' (1995), animation has been particularly suitable for advertising. It immediately provides a different visual aesthetic which may make the advertisement stand out from others; it demonstrates and illustrates (and most often, invents or exaggerates) the properties and capacities of the product; it enables full control over the presentation of the object or artefact, physicalising the non-visual, the non-verbal and the impossible; it transcends taboo issues by virtue of its assumed innocence and fictiveness; it energises otherwise static commodities, creates characters out of them, and makes dynamic reference to the environment and culture within which they exist. Products can be invested with motion, personality, quality and history in a wholly specific way.

Richard Purdum Productions have specialised in this work, using a variety of graphic illusions in 'Smart-i-llusions' to suggest 'Only Smarties have the answer'; echoing Baby Herman in *Who Framed Roger Rabbit* (1988) in their National Dairy Council ad, 'Parents' (1995); metamorphosing a number of modern art forms from Mondrian to Magritte in their 'State of the Art' ad to promote the Tate Gallery, Liverpool (see Wells 1997); and using the lyrical draftsmanship of Oscar-winner Michael Dudok de Wit (*Father and Daughter* (2000)) to illustrate the virtues of recycling in a short film produced for the Chemical Manufacturers Association called 'Recycle' (1995).[3] While there is much invention in these advertisements, they draw upon aesthetic traditions and cultural resources which reflect generic orthodoxies and, once more, while signifying their own status as animation, ostensibly work within the denotative and connotative framework that has been constructed to represent the concept and visual treatment of the product. Essentially, each advertisement prompts its own generic questions. On the one hand, such advertisements reinforce what is already known, while on the other create an insular environment which locates and fixes the product, and simultaneously progresses a view about generic maintenance and renewal. Arguably, it is this notion of maintenance and renewal which animation brings to all generic contexts.

Taylor's categories are useful in narrowing and progressing the ways in which animation in relation to genre may be understood, and in the sense that these perspectives notionally suggest that animation has a set of genres of its own. As we have noted, it seems, however, that this is not wholly satisfactory, and more analysis is required in the attempt to further delineate such genres, and suggest the deep structures that inform them. In many senses this becomes clearer when the orthodox configurations of 'genre' are abandoned and animation is re-thought in another light. While genres like the western, horror or science fiction may be evidenced in animation, as we have demonstrated their credentials become subject to complex interrogations and revisions. Even if there is a further case that animation embraces and evidences the war genre, or the propaganda film, or even Taylor's categories of 'commercials' and 'children's entertainment', it might be equally argued that these are not *pure* genres drawn from the animated canon of films, but rather that they remain distinctive by virtue of their animated techniques and their creative outcomes. Even the concept of maintenance and renewal remains insufficient in some cases, though. The defining generic codes and conventions of a musical, for example, are inappropriate when viewed in relation to animated films. The construction of the soundtrack – songs, music, dialogue, effects and silence – is intrinsic to the creation of all animated films. Animation has no 'natural' diegetic sound; all animation has to self-consciously construct its soundtrack. In some senses this echoes the self-conscious principles which underpin the naturalised artifice of the musical genre – one in which the audience has to accept characters spontaneously bursting into song, and extraordinary acts of choreography and performance occurring, for example, in everyday street scenes. The place of the 'song' and 'dance' is inherent in the very construction of animation. Even Disney features like *Beauty and the Beast* (1992), which effectively echo the conventions of a typical musical, with yearning torch songs and exuberant routines, do so in a spirit of the relationship *between* the sound and the image, rather than in merely the act of recording what is essentially a theatrical performance in live-action cinema. This is the case, therefore, for every sound-synchronised cartoon from *Steamboat Willie* onwards, and causes virtually every animated film – which by necessity might use songs to structure their narratives and to inform their visual currency – to be able to be viewed as a 'musical'. Many early sound-synchronised cartoons, and especially those made by Warner Bros. using the company's music back-catalogue, may be viewed as progenitors of the music video. In order that some perspective can be maintained, and some model of differentiation can prevail, it is important that the role of music and choreography, as it is defined within 'the musical', is not viewed in an over-determining way in relation to animation, because it is clear that it is the integrative nature of song and dance within the aesthetic of the animated form which is its dominant credential, and not its intrinsic relationship to performance. Once more, the principles of the animation become privileged over the generic codes and conventions it relates to, or engages with.

The same argument may be advanced for the 'Romance' or 'Screwball Comedy' – here animation tends to abandon the trials and tribulations of 'boy meets girl', and substitutes cross-species coupling (virtually any Warner Bros. cartoon); cross-dressing (virtually any Bugs Bunny cartoon, but *What's Opera, Doc?* (1957) is seminal); gender-bending (Jerry's role in the 'Tom and Jerry' cartoons); explicit sex (most Bill Plympton films); generational considerations – largely the recovery of relationships between senior citizens (*George and Rosemary* (1984), *Second Class Mail* (1984)); failed romantic bonds (*Pond Life* (1993)); alternative sexualities (*Achilles*); and more surreal takes on human interaction (see Wells 1998; Sandler 1998). Clearly, the terrain explored in vehicles which may be notionally viewed as related to 'romance' moves into different areas of expression and interrogation, largely working as individual treatments, and mostly, implicitly or explicitly using animation to break taboos and make personalised statements which work outside generic resolutions. The key aspect here is in the greater freedoms to address 'the body' in animation, where the physical form is wholly mutable, indestructible, and in some instances, immaterial. Donald Duck can cavort with, and sexually desire, a real woman in *Saludos Amigos* (1942) without anyone particularly noticing or minding; animal characters can regularly appear in drag; masculine and feminine traits can be re-configured and re-contextualised often resulting in the 'camp' performance of sexualities and cultural identities; male erections and sexual acts cease to be taboo; and 'the body' as the central determining factor of generic protagonism is rendered wholly arbitrary. When seen in these ways animation may be understood on its own terms and conditions, and the ways in which its freedoms determine specific kinds of approach are signalled. There may be a case, therefore, to construct 'genres' which seem particular to animation, or at the very least are made distinctive by virtue of using animation as opposed to other forms. For example, the 'fairytale' finds particular purchase in the animated form, largely for three reasons. Firstly, many fairytales are already illustrated in children's books, and have a tradition of illustration which seemingly naturally translates into animated stories. Secondly, the more surreal narrative dynamics and thematic complexities of many fairytales require the more open vocabulary of animation to accommodate them. Thirdly, the fairytale tradition is in many cultures an oral tradition, and the published versions of such fairytales represent the folkloric and mythic pasts of many indigenous groups. Consequently, animation as another form of 'publication' helps to preserve and perpetuate these traditions further. Interestingly, this raises complex issues. Jack Zipes, for example, suggests that:

> It would not be an exaggeration to assert that Disney was a radical film-maker who changed our way of viewing fairytales, and that his revolutionary technical means capitalised on American innocence and utopianism to reinforce the social and political status quo.
> (quoted in Bell *et al.* 1995: 21)

This is a major claim, and one that can be refuted, but what is important here is Disney's implied re-inscribed 'authorship' of these fairytales and the way that they have been 'institutionalised' and translated through animation. Ironically, this echoes the institutionalisation of fairytales *per se* within the literary traditions of most Western cultures, sanitising and expurgating much of the original 'adult' form in a spirit of preparing the tales for the child's nursery. With these translations came a canonisation of particular tales; an emphasis on illustration; narrative resolution in support of socio-cultural orthodoxies; and in general, a denial of the oral tradition. Arguably, even despite Zipes' reservations, it was the animated form that *recovered* this tradition and re-inserted the original tone, complexity and subversiveness of the fairytale. Disney, for example, was responsible for re-engaging with the Grimm brothers' story of 'Snow White and the Seven Dwarfs', when the theatrical version that Disney's original script was based on proved to be too bowdlerised and subject to the same sanitisation as the literary forms were prone to at the end of the nineteenth century (see Merritt in Canemaker 1989). The Fleischer Brothers too, re-visited the 'nightmare' elements of fairytales in the midst of their surreal scenarios. Animation in essence *facilitates* the fairytale because many tales are predicated on metamorphosis and the specificity of particular image forms intrinsic to indigenous cultures and national traditions. *Shrek* (2001) complicates this further by embracing generic aspects of the literary and graphic modes of fairytale, but also offers up a post-modern (and highly amusing) critique of Disney's versions of 'fairytale' and the measured conservatism of their outcomes.

If the fairytale may be viewed as an explicit animated genre, it is not far to the idea of the 'literary adaptation' as especially appropriate to the form. I have argued elsewhere that the 'frame by frame' process in animated film-making has a particular minutiae and specificity of detail that directly echoes the construction of textual description and narrative imperatives, thus providing the most appropriate opportunity to represent the literary text in the most apposite of ways (Wells 1999). Animation provides a particular model of adaptation in that in enunciating itself it foregrounds the concept of *translation*, *transmutation* and *transition* not merely as the vocabulary of the animated form but as the process of taking a literary text and making it a moving picture. The centrality of the idea of 'process' is crucial here, in the sense that if there is to be a view of literary adaptation in the animated form that differs significantly from adaptation in live action, then it is in the way that animation enables the fundamental movement within the text to find ready purchase, literally and metaphorically, in the chosen idiom.

In Joanna Quinn's adaptation of 'The Wife of Bath's Tale' in *The Canterbury Tales*, the animation itself illustrates the central conceptual premises at the heart of the tale. A knight sexually assaults a young woman, but is saved from execution by the intervention of the Queen, who offers him an opportunity to save his life if within the course of a year he can return to her with the answer to the question 'What is the thing that women most desire?' It is pertinent to recall that the underpinning context of courtly romance renders the role of 'wife' subservient, monogamous and physically unalluring, while valuing the 'lover' as young, attractive and sexually uninhibited – essentially the provocateur of the 'beautiful agony' of romantic fulfillment. The knight all but fails to find the answer to his question on his quest until one day when he confronts 24 young women dancing in a leafy glade who, as he approaches them, disappear, leaving only the hunched figure of a skeletal old woman. This is the first evidence of the ethereal, transient and illusory nature of the *idea* of women the

FIGURE 5 *The Wife of Bath's Tale*

knight is attracted to, explicitly depicted in an ethereal, transient and illusory form.

The old woman promises the knight the answer to his question if he will grant her what she wants should he survive. The knight returns to court, and gives the answer that what women most desire is 'sovereignty', in this instance not merely equality in marriage, but for the wife to assume mastery both over her husband and in the resistance to the seemingly naturalised acceptance of his inevitable infidelity. The court accepts his answer and the old woman, to his complete despair, claims his hand in marriage, to which he is forced to agree. Their wedding night sees the old woman chastise her husband for his lack of respect and courtliness, but offer him the choice between a faithful, ugly wife or a young, attractive wanton, who might sleep with other men. Unable to make the choice the knight suggests the old woman make it for him and consequently, winning mastery over him, she criticises his duplicity, promising him that she will be both – in this version chillingly illustrated by an oscillating metamorphosis between voluptuous young lover and skeletal haridan. Quinn's graphic style brings extraordinary vitality to the figures, showing not merely the literal movement of the characters but their psychological and emotional flux as physical states. The final metamorphoses of the loose-limbed grotesque old woman and the physically impassioned young girl vividly shows the ways in which the taken-for-granted typology of 'wife' and 'lover' has been re-configured as a mode of redefinition and empowerment for women, faithful to the tale itself but relevant to contemporary (post)-feminist politics. Further, this is also consistent with Quinn's previous authorial concerns in her films, from *Girls' Night Out* (1986) onwards. Within this generic context animation has, therefore, facilitated both the translation of the literary text into a new form, but just as importantly, the auteurial claims intrinsic to the medium. The *process* of adaptation has once more foregrounded the *process* inherent in animated forms, and consequently, the ways in which animators use, own and control this process in the ways that it actually appears on screen. Quinn's graphic style, sensitivity to translation, and modes of visual storytelling, using the distinctiveness of the form, may be actually witnessed as text, and not deduced from sub-text. Crucially, then, any view of genre in animation must be understood as closely related to animation's ability to announce itself as its own text, which self-evidently interrogates the parameters of its own uses of generic traits and tropes.

As was demonstrated in the previous chapter, this is also the simultaneous re-inscription of the modernist credentials underpinning the form itself. Arguably, all animation works as a version of fine art in motion, and recalls the generic principles which have evolved from art practice. This is important because once again it moves the address of genre in animation away from the iconographic, thematic and narrative concerns which ally the form to its live-action counterpart, and into a view of animation as a practice which is informed by generic 'deep structures'. These structures integrate and counterpoint form and meaning, and further, reconcile approach and application as the *essence* of the art. The generic outcomes of the animated film are imbued in its technical execution. The approach to practice draws upon the history, culture and techniques of fine art, and applies them to conventional approaches to genre in film, both subverting and re-defining genre within live action, and foregrounding the specificity of animation as a process and an engine in the dispersal and dilution of generic orthodoxy. What remains is the *particularity* of animation, and its own conditions of enunciation; conditions which may be understood as deep structures and generic specificities. Inevitably issues arise concerning the applicability of these structures to both feature and short form, but essentially, because of the structural emphasis, it is important to recognise that in any animated form the generic tendency is a matter of emphasis and predominance rather than fixedness. A feature may evidence generic flux because of its structural variousness, for example, but it will remain predominantly in one approach. I have identified seven genres of animated film, which essentially work in this way as approaches to literal, metaphoric, and symbolic 'cycles of movement', and the self-enunciating principle which underpins its aesthetic. These are discussed below.

Formal: Animation that is determined by a conditional premise to its narrative or thematic concerns, in order to test and extend the aesthetic and technical parameters of expression distinctive to the animated form. This may be, for example, the conditions imposed by the recently-deceased Chuck Jones to create a framework for the 'Roadrunner' cartoons (see Jones 1990: 225); the illustration of musical pieces (such as *Fantasia*); a specific visual source (for example Sheila Graber's *William Blake* (1978); a specific soundtrack (such as *Pink Konkommer* (1990)) or the limits imposed by a formalised situation – for example the five figures seeking to possess a musical box standing on an unstable mid-air platform that tips up with any imbalance on the plinth in *Balance* (1989). While not purely formal exercises these pieces work on the basis of the maximum degree of extrapolation from a minimum degree of known tenets. One of the greatest examples of this kind of work is Zbigniew Rybczynski's *Tango* (1982), which is composed of the extended repeated choreography of multiple characters within the confined space of a single room. Each character has a particular role and function, and while never acknowledging each other, they interact through their juxtapositions and symbolic connection. The film thus becomes a rich metaphor for personal and social existence with a high degree of political resonance about the private domain and the public sphere and the oppressive qualities of utilitarian, and potentially authoritarian, routines.

Deconstructive: Animation that reveals the premises of its own construction for critical and comic effects. This informs all the animated film that self-consciously deconstructs the artificial tenets of its making, from Fleischer's *Out of the Inkwell* films to Otto Mesmer's 'Felix the Cat' shorts to Chuck Jones' *Duck Amuck* to Daniel Greaves' *Manipulation*. Arguably all animated films are self-reflexive, but these particular films foreground deconstruction as the subject of their narrative revelations. Any animation which effectively breaks the 'fourth wall' which preserves

FIGURE 6 *Tango*

the integrity of what is a superficially closed-off narrative space and context, and acknowledges the viewer's presence in the act of watching, may also be included in this category. Disney's *Aladdin* (1992), featuring Robin Williams' improvisations as the Genie, directly addressed the audience for one of the few times in Disney's history, and readily echoed the Warner Bros. cartoons in the more adult references used by the character. Bugs and Daffy spoke directly to the viewer; Tex Avery constantly showed the mechanisms of his cartooning (see Wells 1998); while in Walter Santucci's *The Happy Moose* (1995), the foul-mouthed Bronx bull, patterned after Jake La Motta in Martin Scorsese's *Raging Bull* (1980), who improvises a politically-incorrect fairytale for a group of less-than-bright, mixed-race children, admits, like Marlon Brando in *On the Waterfront* (1954): 'I could have been somebody. I could have been a contender, instead of a cartoon, which is what I am...'

Political: Animation which aspires to use the medium to make moral, ethical or political statements. These films have a specific intention and work within the broad parameters of propaganda, public information, educational instruction and social advocacy. They include Disney's wartime feature, *Victory Through Air Power*, illustrating the history of aviation and promoting strategic long-range bombing as the key to winning the war; *Our Friend the Atom* (see M. Langer 1995); health and safety campaigns like the *Charley* series; and a range of environmental films – a topic especially embraced by animators from Les Drew (*What on Earth* (1975)) to Guido Manuli (*Revenge of the Trees* (1993)), to Bruno Bozzetto (*Stop that Car!* (1993)) to William Latham (*Biogenesis* (1993)) to Frédéric Back (*The Mighty River* (1995)).

Abstract: Animation that constructs itself as an abstract material or concrete proposition or interrogation, explicitly exploring new techniques and approaches to facilitate non-objective, non-linear works, or works that resist traditional conventions of understanding and interpretation. These are predominantly experimental films and embrace much of the work of Oskar Fischinger, Norman McLaren, Mary Ellen Bute, Robert Breer and John and James Whitney (see Russett & Starr 1976). These animators have been profoundly influential on numerous artists; for example, McLaren on the multi-styled, mixed-media narratives of Joanna Priestley; Fischinger on Clive Whalley, who extends Fischinger's concerns with colour and form by stressing the energy and glutinous plasticity of paint in the vivid and playful *Slapstick* (1994), which also stresses the artisanal craft orientation of literally 'shaping the world' in the industrial age; and Breer on Stuart Hinton's *Argument in a Supermarket* (1993) which apes Breer's *LMNO* (1978) in its use of simple graphics and fragmented multiple narratives. It is often the very 'materiality' of these works that underpins their stylistic imperatives, simultaneously signaling different orientations in meaning – for example, Anna Fodorova and Vera Neubauer's *La Luna* (1999), with its knitted mice and the revision of 'blood' imagery through the use of unravelling wool.

Re-Narration: Animation which uses the specific and distinctive vocabulary of the form to reconfigure narrative in the representation of time, space, and perspective. Bill Plympton, for example, exemplifies some of the specificities of the animated vocabulary, when in *Plymptoons* he shows evolution in five seconds, depicting a stooping gorilla-like creature metamorphosing into an erect human only to evolve back to the same stooping stance and, by implication, Neanderthal condition, in the form of an American footballer. The extraordinary truncation of time is enabled by using metamorphosis as the determining narrative tool, and such condensation provokes the maximum suggestion to what is essentially the 'story' outcome – the satiric fulfilment of the visual pun. His version of 'a date' in *More Sex and Violence* (1998) shows the inside of a woman's mouth as it devours popcorn at a film, eats dinner, has a kiss, and fellates her companion. The 'date' is defined by the oral functions performed through a passing evening, and is distinctive in the way that it tells its story from this perspective, and in its ultimately daring imagery of an erect penis in the mouth. Again, this could only have been achieved in animation. This aspect also informs stories which effectively improvise characters and events completely beyond the realms of material reality. Again, Walter Santucci's *The Hungry, Hungry Nipples* (1997) features an evil cat, teaming up with 'the flying Richard Nixon Baseball bat' to conquer the violent, milk-squirting nipples, and revive Jean Jean, a boy brutalised by his mother and hurled in the fridge, only to be helped by 'terrorist mustard'. He then discovers his magic capability of using his *Wizard of Oz*-derived red shoes to effect his wants upon the cry of 'Judy Garland was a scabby-arsed heroin addict'. Paul Driessen's *3 Misses* (1998) is perhaps one of the best examples of the 'Re-Narration' model, in taking archetypal plots or plot moments – like a person falling off a building, a woman tied to a railway track, or the seven dwarfs learning that Snow White is to be poisoned – and re-working their previous narrative outcomes. Such narratives not merely advance the traditional kinds of surreality and comic subversion of the cartoon, but revise the meanings of their cultural references.

Paradigmatic: Animation that renders the pre-determined conditions of its making as the foregrounded terms of its construction, and which *may* fulfil the anticipated codes and conventions of established paradigmatic styles and stories. This kind of animation is largely drawn from other, principally literary or graphic narrative sources, but may ultimately be animation which also emerges as a process style in its own right. The former would include SC4/Soyuzmultfilm's *Animated Shakespeare* adaptations, Disney's versions of English literary forms including *Alice in Wonderland* (1951), *Peter Pan* (1953), *101 Dalmations* (1961), and *The Jungle Book* (1967); more personal, interpretive short works like Sarah Downes' *Winter Trees* (1993), a treatment of Sylvia Plath's 1962 poem; and adapted 'strip cartoon' sources like those from Raymond Briggs' 1982 graphic novel, *When the Wind Blows* (1986) (see Kilborn 1986) or *Spawn* (1999). 'Process' style animation would include 'Classic Disney''s predominant aesthetic, but more pertinently, the signature visual definition of animated sit-coms from 'The Simpsons' (1990–present) to 'God, the Devil and Bob' (2000); and children's series from Bob Godfrey's marker-penned 'Roobarb and Custard' (1974–1989) to Cosgrove Hall's mixed model/CGI 'Bill and Ben' (2001). Although there is some variability in sequences and in relation to effects in these works there is a high degree of consistency because of the need for a particular identity in the more highly competitive areas of broadcast markets.

Primal: Animation which depicts, defines and explores a specific emotion, feeling or state of consciousness. This particular aspect of animation can be seen in a variety of works from the underpinning lustful imperatives of Tex Avery's sexually driven wolves to the dreamscapes of Alison de Vere's *The Black Dog* (1987) to the supernatural psycho-babble in David Anderson's *Deadsy*. Arguably, the very condition of the animated film is one which depicts the outcomes of pre-conscious, unconscious and stream-of-consciousness thought through aesthetic applications. Many animations have the tone, style and surreal persuasiveness of the dream or nightmare, and the imagery of recollection, recognition and half-recall. This ambivalent aesthetic has a cognitive status but an ethereal illusiveness; an embedded knowledge but a transient expression. These works often deal with the sensory apparatus, or its denial, as the subject of their text, and occur both in cartoons– for example, Bob Clampett's *The Big Snooze* (1946), which features Bugs putting 'nightmare paint' on Elmer Fudd's dream, and the nude Elmer being overrun by rabbits and chased by wolves while dressed in excessive drag – and in less readily anarchic forms like *Night Angel* (1988), a collaboration between Czech puppeteer Bratislav Pojar and pinscreen specialist, Jacques Drouin, which combines the two forms in a way that a man's temporary blindness following an accident sees him trapped between illusion and reality, hope and despair as he remains uncertain of his worldly status. Yuri Norstein's *Tale of Tales* (see Wells 1998; Wells 2001a) is perhaps the definitive 'primal' animation film in that it is a combination of meditation, memory, dream and heightened consciousness, and best illustrates the applied and aesthetic parameters of animation as a distinctive form of cinema itself.

These seven generic 'deep structures' are offered as a point of departure in the debates about genre in animation, and should be understood as provisional engagements with the issue. In many senses, the discussion of these principles anticipates similar complexities in the discussion of 'authorship' which follows in the next chapter, and should be taken into account as relevant underpinning aspects of authorial approaches and concerns.

5 THE ANIMATION AUTEUR

The issue of authorship in film-making practice has proved to be an area of contention and dispute throughout film history. The very term 'authorship' retains strong connotations of its literary source, and the affirmative culture of 'high art'. It was a context with which the French film-makers and critics of the *Cahiers du Cinéma* – among them François Truffaut, Jean-Luc Godard and Claude Chabrol – sought to underpin their use of the term 'auteur' in their pioneering work of the 1950s, which properly credited significant but unsung individual film-makers, with an identifiable signature style, who were making important films within the assumed generic and industrial homogeneity of the Hollywood studio system (see Caughie 1993). The writers for *Movie* in Britain, and Andrew Sarris in the United States, nuanced the debates further. Auteurist film-makers, in creating a distinctive 'text', were accorded the legitimacy and authority of their literary forebears, and distinguished from the mere competency of the 'jobbing' *metteur en scène*. An auteurist director was recognised as having a unique signatory impramature across a canon of work, that marked out an aesthetic and thematic terrain, and offered a coherent view of the discourses fundamental to its understanding and 'art'.

The collaborative and process-oriented nature of much film-making practice became subordinate to the critical parameters that determined film as a director's medium and directors as the significant 'voice' of the film. The role of the screenwriter, the cinematographer, and the actor – to name but the most obvious – was subjugated to the authorial claims of the director, and comparatively few film historians and critics have privileged these contributory figures and their roles as serious challengers to the pre-eminence of the director as the romantic conception of the 'artist' at the heart of the predominantly industrial and commercial practices of contemporary film production. Clearly, numerous directors do have very clear credentials which support the view that their vision, integrity and expertise do validate their status as auteurs, but few operate in a spirit by which their work can be singularly delineated, or extricated from the profoundly influential contributions of others in the creation of their work. Even as great a director as Martin Scorsese, for example, has benefited from the screenwriting presence of Paul Schrader, the credibility and authenticity of Robert de Niro's acting, and the expertise of Thelma Schoonmaker's editing, and these aspects must be acknowledged if the exemplariness of his best achievements may be properly understood as 'art'.

Inevitably, no definitive account of authorship in cinematic practice is possible, and the discussion of the nature of authorship remains problematic, coloured by a range of debates which at one level can invest directors with an almost God-like omnipotence and influence, while on another dismiss their relevance almost entirely. The former model insists upon the artistic prominence of the director; the latter suggests that once the filmic text is given over to its audience it is only their interpretation of, and interpellation with, the text that matters, effectively marginalising the director's intentions, interventions and achievements (see Barthes 1984: 142–8). This in itself means that other factors like narrative, genre, star-presence, effects and so forth may be a more meaningful indicator of the status of the work than its director. The industry still 'sells' a director as a commercial verifier of a work; fans still valorise particular figures who represent a coherent view of a style, theme or genre; academics still publish monographs celebrating and re-discovering auteurs – effectively the nature of authorship still remains a valid and complex site of shifting paradigms and tensions.

Animation further problematises the issue of authorship in the sense that on the one hand it echoes and imitates the terms and conditions of large-scale industrial film production processes, while on the other offers the possibility for a film-maker to operate almost entirely alone. Arguably, animation may be viewed as the most auteurist of film practices in this respect, and its very process, even when at its most collaborative, insists upon the cohesive intervention of an authorial presence. Interestingly, however, few directors are lauded as auteurs in relation to American feature-length animation, with their identities subsumed within a corporate identity (such as 'Disney'), or to the generic appeal of the narrative, characters and so forth, or the implicit acceptance of the collaborative process in the creation of the final artefact. The latter aspect is interesting in the sense that it emerges out of the received knowledge of animation as a complex and time-consuming process, that seemingly differs from similarly complex processes of collaboration in live-action cinema. Related to this is the persistent view that animation is predominantly for a children's audience, and that its authorship is irrelevant to such a demographic. It is important, therefore, to recover the debates about authorship and apply them to the variety of approaches in the field of animation. As was discussed, there are a number of models of animated film production, and almost as many variations in the ways that the practitioners making animated films may be viewed as auteurs. It is worthwhile, therefore, identifying a range of possible positions which speak to a definition of the auteur, and then applying them to these particularities. These definitions may be divided into two broad areas: *Textual* and *Extra-Textual*, although inevitably these areas overlap and intersect, and will be embedded in the discussion that follows.

Textual

The auteur may be understood as:

- a person who prompts and executes the core themes, techniques and expressive agendas of a film.
- a figure around whom the key enunciative techniques and meanings of a film accrue and find implied cohesion.
- a figure who provides the organising principles of textual practices to engage with, and create motivated spectatorial positions.
- a person who offers direct statements and explanations about the artistic and thematic intentions of a film, within an evolving 'narrative' about the film-maker from work to work, which constitutes a personal vision.
- a figure who is an implied presence in the narrative of a film, enunciating its textual and sub-textual imperatives.
- a commercial, critical and cultural construction of coherence and consistency in creative contexts where none may exist.
- an agent who foregrounds the relationship between, and the material conditions of, art and commerce as the underpinning

imperative of the approach (by working in recognised formulas, narrative practices, genres, SFX orientations, and so on).

- a mediating figure between the pragmatic processes of the film industry and the complex expectations and reactions of the audience.
- an agent for the recovery of a nexus of previous films, genres, approaches et cetera.
- the persona of 'subjectivity' within the text, and extra-textually, embodying the historical and socio-cultural determinants that underpin the work (a political movement, a producer of propaganda, information, and so on).
- a 'sign' or 'structure' which represents the presiding imperatives of the *mise-en-scène*, narrative and theme in a film or series of films.

Extra-Textual

The auteur may be understood as:

- a figure who embodies a coherent position about a film which makes complex production processes invisible, and obscures or inhibits an alternative view about the authorially determined claims of others in the execution of the film.
- a historically adaptable idea which offers a way of implying and understanding how a film should be received.
- a 'romantic' concept suggesting an elevated role within a mass entertainment medium that may be related to already established and authentic modes of authorship in classical and high art models, and also operating as a sign of differentiation from other forms of mass media (such as television, radio, web-casting, and so on).
- a method of aesthetically and culturally sanctioning the quality of the work.
- a way of legitimising, authenticating and stabilising critical reception.
- an approach to 'branding' a film within the commercial imperatives of late industrial capitalism.
- an approach which uses the authorial figure to represent the 'art' in a film in order to differentiate and distanciate it from the less elevated imperatives of 'commerce' that drive its making.

- a method by which to read a film, or series of films, with coherence and consistency, over-riding all the creative diversity, production processes, socio-cultural influences and historical conditions et cetera which may challenge this perspective.
- a maintenance of the ideology of the 'freedom of the artist'.
- a mode of mass mediated celebrity/personality which sometimes overrides the significance or quality of the film, but fulfils the needs of cultural consumption.
- an institutional structure which operates as a 'pre-condition' to the film, suggesting that an audience might already 'know' the film, without having wholly 'read' it. Cynically, this might be viewed as 'consumption' without 'reception'.
- the embodiment and epitome of independent, original and potentially subversive vision in art, in support of the 'genius' myth.
- a challenger to corporate, institutional and systemic oppression and coercion.
- a figure that self-consciously defines 'auteurism' against other perspectives.
- a figure constructed within the remit of film criticism, which legitimised the serious study of Hollywood film in the same spirit as art-house or independent work.
- an inhibiting and inappropriate 'construct' which denies the strengths of the industrial context of the studio system; which limits the debate about the 'authorial' agenda in film-making practice; and which values and promotes the consistency of the authorial signature over the individual quality of a film, either made by the 'auteur' or another, less renowned film-maker.

These perspectives are drawn from a wide range of critical positions but serve to provide a vocabulary by which the following case studies in animation may be addressed. Each of these – Walt Disney, Ray Harryhausen, and Caroline Leaf – are chosen to represent three different approaches to the definition of authorship within animation, and equally, to serve as an extended discussion of the particularities of animation as a form situated within these debates and parameters. Clearly, one of the most complex and important figures in these debates is Walt Disney, the most well-known and influential figure in the field; his studio, nearly forty years after his death, still the most dominant force in the animation industry in the contemporary era.

Walt Disney

Walt Disney is viewed as the key pioneering figure in the creation of the art, commerce and industry of animation. He is the most written-about figure in the field, both at the personal level, and as the embodiment of a studio, a brand, and an ethos (see Holliss & Sibley 1988; Smoodin 1994; Wasko 2001). Disney himself has been both canonised as the epitome of the promise, value and achievement underpinning the American Dream, and castigated as ideologically unsound and politically incorrect; a racist and a petty, artless, businessman. His life has inevitably been entwined with his art; his entrepreneurial flair either embraced as intrinsically American and wholly appropriate to modern commercial enterprise, or as the trait which marks him out as a money-maker instead of a Monet or a Mondrian. Even his fiercest advocates, however, have struggled to name Disney's mode of authorship, and it is quite clear that this operates as a useful case study by which to address the claims made by his biographers, promoters and critics, and to form a view of the ways 'authorship' in animation might be evaluated.

Disney himself suggested: 'I think of myself as a little bee. I go from one area of the studio to another and gather pollen and sort of stimulate everybody ... that's the job I do' (quoted in Schickel 1987: 33). Disney recognised that he played a role in his own studio which was difficult for the public to understand, because although he was the named author of the work, he did not actually *draw* any of the material his audiences saw, and it was this that the public viewed as the intrinsic difference of a cartoon from its live-action counterpart. Its 'magic' lay in its apparent transparency as a medium; these were drawings that moved. The logical assumption is to believe that the name attached to the cartoon was the person who executed the drawings; an assumption that was already proven incorrect, for example, by the fact that studio head Pat Sullivan took credit for the 'Felix the Cat' cartoons, when they were wholly conceived and executed by Otto Messmer. Interestingly, Disney did start out making and drawing his own cartoons in the *Newman Laugh-O-Grams* of the 1920s, animating, among others, fairytales like *Little Red Riding Hood* (1922), *The Four Musicians of Bremen* (1922), *Jack and the Beanstalk* (1922) and *Puss in Boots* (1922), before graduating to his animated, part live-action series of *Alice* cartoons, for which he animated only seven films, including *Alice's Wonderland* (1923), *Alice Hunting in Africa* (1923), *Alice's Wild West Show* (1924) and *Alice the Dog Catcher* (1924), before putting

FIGURE 7 Mickey Mouse

down his pencil and concentrating on story and direction, passing the actual animation on to Ub Iwerks and Rollin Hamilton. Schickel notes of this period, however, that:

> Disney's drive for technical perfection, one of the most important elements in his career, manifested itself early. He did all the animation himself, of course, functioned as director and cameraman on the live sequences and even constructed the sets single-handed. (Schickel 1986: 105)

Disney himself recalled:

> I started as an artist in 1919. And I actually did my first animated films in early 1920. And at that time I drew everything, painted every background and things. And I carried along as an animator and an artist until about the time of Mickey Mouse. Now when Mickey Mouse came along there was such a demand – he made quite a

> splash – [that] it was necessary then for me to give up the drawing in order to organise and run the organisation.[1]

This moment may be viewed as a pivotal transition from one mode of authorship to another in the sense that, quite simply, he moves from *actually* making the films to facilitating their production. While some would argue that this relinquishes the most applied model of authorship in animation, it does not, however, undermine Disney's claims to authorship at another level, in the sense that Disney, to choose from our taxonomy, still operated as 'a person who prompts and executes the core themes, techniques and expressive agendas of a film'. Equally, this moment does prompt the view that the role that Ub Iwerks played in the development of the *Alice* cartoons, and ultimately, the stylistic distinctiveness of the *Silly Symphonies*, needs further evaluation, as it is the *visual* currency of the cartoon which defines its significance and difference. The *Silly Symphonies* were of a different, more progressive, graphic order and quality than the cartoons that preceded them, with the possible exception of the work of Winsor McCay, but arguably, their distinctiveness was not only visual, and importantly, they benefited from Disney's intervention at the level of characterisation, storytelling and 'gag' construction. By taking into account Iwerks' contribution, however, it is possible to challenge the view that Disney can be wholly understood as 'a figure around whom the key enunciative techniques and meanings of a film accrue and find implied cohesion'. Michael Barrier has suggested that:

> [Iwerks] could have made a strong claim to stand on an equal footing with Walt as a creator of cartoons, and any such claim would have had a legal dimension because Iwerks was part-owner of the studio. [Carl] Stalling [Disney's musical collaborator], too, could have made claims that came with ownership – he had invested $2,000 in a separate Disney Film Recording Company – and, like Iwerks, he had resisted accommodating himself completely to Walt's demands ... After Iwerks and Stalling left, Walt Disney was for the first time working only with collaborators who were unequivocally subordinate to him. (Barrier 1999: 67)

In many senses, the relationship between Disney, Iwerks and Stalling represents the first small-scale yet complex discourse about the nature of authorship, but one rooted in the analysis of the production of the texts. Arguably, once Iwerks and Stalling stopped working with Disney, and Disney was able to establish a hierarchical infrastructure that placed himself as the key instigator and producer of the work, he moved onto a plane in which his role may be understood extra-textually. For example, by the late 1920s, it is possible to suggest that he had become 'a figure who embodies a coherent position about a film which makes complex production processes invisible, and obscures or inhibits an alternative view about the authorially determined claims of others in the execution of the film'. Once Disney consolidated his studio practice and ethos, this position did not change, and 'animation' itself comes to be defined as a mode of film-making, both obscuring and denying its historical antecedents, and the particular claims to and definitions of authorship which may be drawn from the work of such figures as McCay, Messmer, Paul Terry, Raoul Barré, Charles Bowers, and the Fleischer Brothers in the American context, and significant others like Emile Cohl and Landislaw Starewich elsewhere.

Contemporary historians and critics have to some degree rectified this by recovering the work of these figures, and acknowledging its proper place, prioritising, for example, in the *Felix the Cat* cartoons, a case for Messmer, again from our taxonomy, 'as the agent of textual distinctiveness' (see Canemaker 1996); and in relation to McCay's inclusion of the *Gertie the Dinosaur* (1914) cartoon in his vaudeville act, arguing for McCay as 'a figure who provides the organising principles of textual practices to engage with, and create, motivated spectatorial positions' (see Canemaker 1987).

Disney's imperatives were of a different, and more developed, order. He did not only wish to make films, but to make commercially viable films in a technologically advanced, modern industrial context, which could challenge the output of the established studios *and* make claims to being a distinctive art form. As Janet Wasko has noted: 'What is also overlooked in many of the Disney histories is how small the company actually was by comparison with the corporate giants that controlled the film industry at the time' (Wasko 2001: 12). This led Disney to constantly prompt technological development in the promotion of his aim, achieving sound synchronisation ahead of the Fleischer Brothers in *Steamboat Willie*. As Barrier has noted, Disney's use of bar sheets to facilitate synchronisation for the film 'gave Disney, as director, unprecedented control over the animation's timing' (Barrier 1999: 51). His 'insistence on marrying sound and image as tightly as possible paid off in what was instantly recognisable as a real sound cartoon, rather than a silent cartoon with an added soundtrack' (Barrier 1999: 55). Disney also introduced Technicolor into the cartoon in *Flowers and Trees* (1932); developed the multi-plane camera to enhance realist perspectives in the graphic idiom in *The Old Mill*, and culminated these achievements with the first, full-length, sound-synchronised, colour animated cartoon with *Snow White and the Seven Dwarfs*. The 1930s had consolidated the Disney Studio, advanced the credentials of its charismatic leader, initiated the 'Disney' brand, symbolised by Disney's signature – actually a designed version of his name which he learned to copy – and defined animation as an art. Disney, too had successfully created a division of labour in his studio which successfully facilitated the industrial production of animated cartoons in a near cost-effective way, although Disney's profound ambition to advance the studio's work resulted in financial difficulties on many occasions. Disney's success in this respect must not be understated because he, in effect, recognised that the animation industry lagged behind the other studios by not having a viable production infrastructure, and if the form itself was to succeed in becoming a popular form, and a form which would consolidate and advance its own artistic credentials and distinctiveness, it needed to have the same professionalism as its competitors. By 1940 Disney was acknowledged by journalist Paul Hollister as 'the spark plug of production. No story starts toward a picture until Walt has bought it or invented it, shaped it, tried it out, and given it a push ... his authority signalled when he suggested to his animators "Don't look to me for the answers ... all I want you to use me for is approval"' (Hollister 1994: 38). Self-evidently, Disney's model of authorship has changed significantly.

Consequently, Alan Bryman suggests that 'Walt Disney [belongs] ... to a category of charismatic leaders/entrepreneurs who dream up a vision about the need for a product, attract others to that vision and build the organisation into an enthusiastic group of adherents' (Bryman 1995: 14). Schickel adds:

> Looking back, it is easy to see that Disney was neither a sold-out nor a sidetracked artist. He was a man who had obtained what he truly wanted: elevation – at least on the lower levels – to the ranks of other great inventor-entrepreneurs in our industrial history. He was the stuff of Ford and Edison: a man who could do everything a great entrepreneur is expected to do – dream and create and hold. (Schickel 1986: 38)

These insights helpfully support a view of Disney as 'an agent who foregrounds the relationship between, and the material conditions of, art and commerce as the underpinning imperative of the approach'. While Disney was a serial innovator technologically, his real vision was to advance the storytelling conditions and imperatives in animation, and to insist upon the technical expertise which could best facilitate the execution of motion and gesture to support sustainable notions of 'personality' in animated forms. It was Disney who recognised that his animators needed training in support of this ambition and, in effect, allied industrial imperatives to the educational principles of an art school. This made animation a *sophisticated* art form; one in which it was necessary to acquire not merely skills and expertise, but long-term practice. This elevated the sketch, the comic strip, the caricature, the cartoon, and the graphic arts in general, beyond their populist, ephemeral conditions, and insisted upon their craft and the quality of their execution. Contentiously, Disney claimed the credit for the outcomes of this process because he initiated and facilitated it; he was the author of the process, thus the progenitor of its consequences. This inevitably caused some degree of conflict. As Robin Allan notes:

> Disney's determination to assert his name is linked with his obsession with control and quality of product. It has often been noted and the following comment is typical: 'When I first joined the studio, Walt took me on one side and said, "If you have any idea about making a name for yourself, get out. I'm the only star here".' (Ken Anderson, quoted in Allan 1999: 34)

Michael Barrier observes that:

> The writers, in particular, more than the animators, whose work typically came before Disney free of any confusion about authorship, believed they had to find ways to capture Disney's attention, not just for what they had done, but for themselves. Thus Joe Grant broke with the prevailing pattern by using colour in his story sketches. (Barrier 1999: 137)

Clearly, Disney's staff fully recognised that they both had to impress Disney with the originality and progressiveness of their approach, while accepting it would then be subsumed, unacknowledged, within his vision. This culture of appropriation was challenged by Art Babbitt, one of the key figures in the Disney Strike of 1941 who perhaps not unsurprisingly – given the treatment he endured from the Disney Studio – notes of Disney: 'He had no knowledge of draftsmanship, no knowledge of music, no knowledge of literature. Walt himself was not an artist ... but he was a good critic, and could spot if something was wrong, and he was a great editor.'[2] Another of Disney's most senior animators, and one of the 'Nine Old Men' since named as the key figures of the 'Golden Era' between 1928 and 1941, Ward Kimball consolidates this view further:

> We had a little movieola projector so you could run [the film] back and forth. And he'd say, 'run it back – do you see where he puts his foot down, he's not really making contact'. He couldn't draw very well but he knew what was wrong. He knew if a gag wasn't being put over properly ... You took [the criticism] because he was the Boss. If you didn't take it, you were fired. You never overlooked the fact that he had this terrific sense of story, and staging a plot or a gag – he was a great gag man. He was also a pantomimist. If he was asked to do it in public, he would refuse, he couldn't. But when he wound up explaining, for example, how the dwarves would react, he would immediately go into each one of the characters, and we used to say that he was just as good at it as Chaplin.[3]

These perspectives radically return Disney to the 'text', in the sense that he is operating in what may be regarded as a more traditional directorial role, although in the context of animation this is concerned with enabling those who are facilitating the execution of character action in scenes to understand their work, not merely in the context of the creation of movement in the moment, but within the fullest extent of the narrative or comic imperative of the character overall. Further, although Babbitt may deny Disney's personal artistic and cultural credentials, Disney's assurance about the film *he* is in principle making enables him to make authorial decisions and corrections on behalf of others, drawing the fullest potential from his artists in the execution of *his* vision. Speaking in 1963, Disney articulated his view clearly:

> The kind of films I make, I do them because I like to make them. I just wouldn't feel right trying to do some off-beat thing. I don't like the down-beat. When I go to a movie, I don't like to go and see something that leaves me depressed. I basically make films to

> satisfy myself and, of course, my severest critics are right there in my organisation. I have to fight them sometimes. They say 'Well now look, this isn't Disney,' and I say, 'Well, wait a minute, I'm Disney and I buy it'. I make my films for the public and I'll stand judgement before the public. You know, an honest person, to me, is someone that can really sit down and not be afraid to show a little emotional reaction to something, or not be afraid to go back to his childhood. These are the honest people. I don't care what the critics say. Critics sometimes lose contact with the public.[4]

In this respect, Disney's authorial claims may be evaluated in their most obvious way. He may be seen as 'a person who offers direct statements and explanations about the artistic and thematic intentions of a film, within an evolving narrative about the film-maker from work to work, which constitutes a personal vision'. Here Disney validates his own ownership of the film texts and more importantly suggests some of the motives which drive the making of the films, and hint at their content. Disney trusts his own understanding of the public, and the ways his films speak to their potential needs. He stresses the 'emotional' centre of the narratives, and the innocence and engagement of childhood perspectives and perception. Arguably, it was this which Disney insisted upon in his art above the imperatives of his artists, who wished to bring other aspects to the production which Disney viewed as inappropriate.

This is one of the strongest credentials in the argument for Disney's auteurist position, in the sense that he resists anything, both in the production of the film and in its critical reception, which does not accord with his view of the integrity of the work in relation to its audience. Disney knew that he had created the 'art' of animation by mobilising the highest quality skills and techniques in its production within an industrial model. Thereafter, he could seek out its audience through traditional storytelling, persuasive characters, personality-driven scenarios and folk humour, trusting that the public was in accord with populist politics and utopian ambition, and what ultimately would be regarded as 'Classic Disney' (see Watts 1997). His acknowledged authorship becomes 'a way of legitimising, authenticating and stabilising critical reception' in the sense that the 'Disney' imprimatur prompts the critical engagement that, ironically, also calls into question the nature of authorial outcomes. This is especially interesting in the case of Disney, because it is a response that has been sustained in the period following his death in 1966.

Critics have had to come to terms with Disney's longevity, and re-inscribe both Disney the individual, and Disney the studio brand, with a range of meanings which both inform and transcend all the contexts that represent 'Disney' across its history into the present day. Consequently, each new discussion of Disney has to address the inevitable consistencies of the studio-endorsed biographies of Disney by Frank Thomas and Leonard Mosley; the self-mythologisation of Disney himself throughout his long career in film-making and broadcasting; the film texts from *Steamboat Willie* to *The Emperor's New Groove* (2001); the television programmes and The Disney Channel; the merchandising; the Theme Parks and so on. In relation to the film aspects of this process, Robin Allan argues that:

> Until the mid-fifties Walt Disney remained personally involved in all stages of production, and in particular during the collectively creative period when stories and ideas were being thrashed out in committee; it can be said that he was, if not the auteur, then the controlling editor. (Allan 1999: 1)

This is to once again argue for a view of Disney authorship which operates as 'a sign or structure which represents the presiding imperatives of the *mise-en-scène*, narrative and theme in a film, or series of films'. While this enables a discussion about Disney films which may be able to discern their consistent preoccupations and themes, it remains difficult to interpret both the animated shorts and features as 'personal' films. I have argued elsewhere that the term 'Disney' be re-defined as a metonym for *an authorially complex, hierarchical industrial process, which organises and executes selective practices within the vocabularies of animated film* (see Davies & Wells 2001). This view is adopted in order to recover the areas discussed here as key issues in the debate about Disney and authorship, but also to prioritise an address of the aesthetic agendas of the Disney canon in preference to ideological debates. This may also be a corrective, too, for the idea that Disney the man can be read directly through the films as if they were specifically 'personal'. This kind of reading, for example, is at the heart of Marc Eliot's controversial biography of Disney, which seeks to recover allegedly less palatable aspects of Disney's personality and lifestyle, and play them out through the texts. He notes that 'Disney's conflicted inner-self ... inspired so much of his art' (Eliot 1994: xxii), adding, when commenting upon Disney's effusive obituaries:

> Overlooked in the many tributes were his role in the formation of the Hollywood Alliance and its vigilante-like intimidation of those it considered subversive; his friendly testimony before the House of Un-American Activities Committee; his lifelong fear of illegitimacy and his search for the woman he believed to have been his real mother; his 25 years of undercover work for the FBI; his virulent anti-union activities; his association with organised crime; and his relentless obsession with putting to an end to what he believed was a studio system led by a band of corrupt Jewish European immigrants. (Eliot 1994: xxii)

Read in conjunction with the films, such perspectives may significantly alter the way that Disney's authorship may be defined and understood, as it is clear that the reading of the texts may be skewed by this alleged knowledge of the 'personality' that created them. While this mode of auteurism has enjoyed considerable purchase, it returns analysis to the model where the auteur is understood 'as the persona of subjectivity within the text, and extra-textually, embodying the historical and socio-cultural determinants that underpin the work'. This kind of reading, along with the approaches which see only misrepresentation, socio-cultural insensitivity, and ideological malpractice (see Bell *et al* 1995; Giroux 1997; Byrne & McQuillan 1999), tends to focus only on the deconstruction and re-interpretation of the text at the expense of evaluating the complexity of the animation process, which effectively subverts, or at least challenges, such coherence. The problem which arises from this is a tendency to view 'Disney' – the man, the studio, the brand – 'as an institutional structure which operates as a pre-condition to the film, suggesting that an audience might already 'know' the film, without having wholly 'read' it.' This enables critics to suggest that audiences only view Disney films at the level of their 'narrative' and not in relation to their 'text'. Consequently, they suggest, the audience misses the unacceptable and inappropriate meanings perpetrated either by Disney the man, or Disney the corporate oppressor. Significantly, audiences do not readily seem to acknowledge or be affected by the unacceptable aspects supposedly imbued in the texts during Disney's own 'hands-on' interventions, or inscribed in the texts after his death, largely endorsing the idea of the films as persuasive, non-politicised entertainments (see Wells 1998; Wasko 2001).

What remains crucial in this debate is the role of animation itself. Disney was committed to strong storytelling with highly provocative emotional charges and assurances, and insisted upon the quality of animation which would succeed in achieving these goals. This inevitably prioritises *how* the story is told, and to a certain extent *why* the story is told, as it is necessary to establish the objectives for the movement of the characters in specific scenarios and scenes. Such is the multiple collaborative nature of making an animated film of this sort. Therefore, it is highly contestable whether anything but archetypal meanings and effects remain at the textual level, which in principle, Disney would have known, promoted and endorsed. Any idea that the biographical imperatives, suggested by Eliot – conscious or unconscious – could survive such a process is highly questionable. Further, although the Disney studios did produce effective propaganda during World War Two, this was grounded in overt conditions which required that messages were clear and unequivocal in support of the war effort. The emotional and morally-charged aspects of Disney's normal film-making practices were rooted in traditional storytelling practices which benefited from their exposition and explication through the freedoms of the animated vocabulary. The 'openness' of the animation language is thus ambivalent and contradictory. On the one hand, it can support the claims for authorial 'fingerprints' in relation to the 'personality' of its creator, or ideological coherence in relation to its studio's production context and market imperatives, at the textual level. On the other hand, it can refute these claims because of the complexity of the industrial production processes, and the specificity of their outcomes in this type of orthodox animation (see Wells 1998).

It is worth considering that process a little further, in the sense that issues of ownership and control can precede the text, but ultimately affect it very directly. In relation to Disney, this is especially pertinent with regard to the adaptation of other literary sources, and the so-called 'Disnification' of the texts. Schickel argues:

> Even when he began buying literary properties from writers outside his organisation, as feature-length animation and live-action feature projects virtually forced him to do, he did everything in his power to make the original story and characters his own. Part of this was accidental: his well-geared merchandising organisation, with its many 'versions' of original stories like *Bambi* and *Mary Poppins* (designed to catch all age groups) and with its intensive programme of licensed dolls, toys and games based on the subjects, had a natural tendency to blanket the original. But part of it was anything

> but accidental. Disney naturally got credit above the title and in far larger type than the original author, who could not get a contract from the organisation without agreeing to submit his creations to the merchandising process. (Schickel 1986: 113)

Here, Disney uses the inscription of his specific style of animation to subjugate appropriate stories to his authorial presence and interpretation, operating in a way 'which uses the authorial figure to represent the 'art' in a film in order to differentiate and distanciate it from the less elevated imperatives of 'commerce' that drive its making', and further, at its most diminishing to the author, and most advantageous to 'Disney', as 'a method by which to read a film, or series of films, with coherence and consistency, overriding all the creative diversity, production processes, socio-cultural influences and historical conditions et cetera which may challenge this perspective'. This not merely demotes and sometimes absents the original writer of the story – for example, Lewis Carroll (*Alice in Wonderland*); Carlo Collodi (*Pinocchio*); Dodie Smith (*101 Dalmations*) – but also those who should be credited with its production, as it is they who are actually enacting the process of 'Disnification' which is effectively substituting one narrative and textual imperative for another, in order to conform to a normative condition of animation substantially created by Disney. Again, Disney's claims to authorship are concerned with the ownership of an aesthetic which is not undermined or challenged by its visual or literary sources.

Disney removed himself from technical comment to the more objective directorial position which tried to envisage the clarity of story, execution of gags and so on from the perspective of the audience, and with this promoted the shift from 'rubber hose' characters – pioneered by Bill Nolan in 1915, but advanced by Ub Iwerks in the early Disney shorts – and graphic gag pictures – Messmer's 'Felix the Cat' cartoons, for example – to situational humour within storytelling premises. In this he significantly benefited from the work of Norm Ferguson who, as early as *Frolicking Fish* (1930), facilitated the kind of movement in characters whereby different parts of a body could be moving in different directions and at different speeds. This enabled a profoundly important development in Disney's desire to achieve naturalism in character action. Ferguson's use of 'overlapping action' promoted an illusion of lifelike action rather than a slavish imitation of it, and consequently created one of the key aspects of the Disney aesthetic.

Don Graham, the main teacher at the Disney-affiliated Chouinard School of Art, insisted upon this kind of analytical approach to movement and its intrinsic relationship to personality and character, and further to the action required by the narrative. Arguably, therefore, Fred Moore's work on *Three Little Pigs* (1933), in being the synthesis of character animation in the 'squash 'n' stretch' style, fluid storytelling, and comic business, was also instrumental in defining 'Disney' in anticipation of the full-length features later. This aesthetic was sometimes challenged by the work of Art Babbitt and Hamilton Luske, who resisted the movement towards 'cute' by seeking greater verisimilitude in shorts like *The Pied Piper* (1933). By 1932, Disney had three director/composer teams – David Hand and Bert Lewis; Burt Gillett (later replaced by Ben Sharpsteen) and Frank Churchill; and Wilfred Jackson and Leigh Harline, and these couplings were essentially instrumental in making the cartoon shorts. Burt Gillett's *Playful Pluto* (1934) is a tour-de-force of animation facilitated by Norm Ferguson, as it properly showed the relationship between the inner life of Pluto's character and its external consequences. The slapstick emerges from the actions and reactions of Pluto's character. Disney's 'authorship' is most under question in these specific instances because what was achieved was a direct result of those who actually made it, and not the imposition of editorial control.

The role of the director still remains important, of course, but Disney did not direct many of the *Silly Symphonies*, and when he did – as in *The Golden Touch* (1935) – he singularly failed to create a cartoon like David Hand's *Who Killed Cock Robin?* (1935) and *Pluto's Judgement Day* (1935) which, as Barrier has observed 'gave Disney better films than Disney had been able to make himself' (Barrier 1999: 138). Further, as Eliot notes:

> Although Walt had 'directed' some of the earlier 'Alices' and was, in effect, the 'director' of his first cartoons, *The Golden Touch* was his first 'official' directing effort, and looked it. The continuity was choppy, the storytelling preachy, the dialogue pretentious. Walt, in one last attempt to show the king was really a regular guy, ended the film having him going out for a hamburger ... *The Golden Touch* marked the beginning and end of Walt's directing career. (Eliot 1994: 81–2)

Regardless of this, Disney transcended any of the orthodox roles in film-making practice to operate as 'a figure around whom the key enunciative techniques and meanings of a film accrue and find implied cohesion'. Walt represented more than the sum of the parts of his film-making practice by denying the actual achievement of the parts. Disney himself suggested:

> We have but one thought, and that is for good entertainment. We like to have a point to our stories, not an obvious moral but a worth-while theme. Our most important aim is to develop definite personalities in our cartoon characters ... We invest them with life by endowing them with human weaknesses which we exaggerate in a humourous way. Rather than a caricature of individuals, our work is a caricature of life. (quoted in Schickel 1987: 174)

The proprietorial 'we' is significant because Disney's auteurial status resides on his own personal sense of ownership and control of the outcomes of his studio's work. While Douglas Gomery may correctly claim that 'we are fools if we ascribe all the actions and strategies of a company to one man or woman' and that 'the Disney company is simply another capitalist enterprise with a history best understood within the changing conditions of twentieth-century America' (Gomery 1994: 72–3), it is clearly the case that throughout his career and ironically, even after his death, Walt Disney is an auteur by virtue of fundamentally denying inscription to anyone else, and creating an identity and a mode of representation which, despite cultural criticism, market variations, and changing social trends, transcends the vicissisitudes of contemporary America.

Ray Harryhausen

Since his retirement from active film-making in 1982, Ray Harryhausen has been rightly lauded for his achievements and influence in the field of stop-motion animation. This period has seen a recovery of his work as technically innovative, aesthetically ground-breaking, and highly distinctive in its visual style. Harryhausen's 'narrative' – the influence of, and collaboration with Willis O'Brien; the period with European 'replacement animation' master George Pal working on his seminal *Puppetoons*; the transition from his own short films, the *Mother Goose Fairytales*, to becoming an effects supremo on a range of 1950s 'B' movies; the working partnership with producer Charles Schneer on fantasy features; and the post-retirement valorisation – has now been long-established in his own public appearances, and in the eyes of the third generation of 'movie-brat' film-makers who follow in his wake – Joe Dante, James Cameron, and Dennis Muren. This 'narrative' has largely been informed by the desire of critics and fellow animators to promote Harryhausen's status as an auteur within the variety of contexts in which he has worked: firstly, in a spirit of recognising his achievements within a particular approach to animation; secondly, in order to profile his work, essentially made 'invisible' within an American effects tradition; and thirdly, to recognise the specificity of his claims to a quasi-directorial role within films wholly predicated on the centrality of his work to the premise and execution of the narratives. Drawing on the taxonomy above, Harryhausen is clearly 'a figure around whom the key enunciative techniques and meanings of a film accrue and find implied cohesion', with a particular emphasis upon the way that the technique facilitates the meaning of the films by enabling them to have a different and appealing aesthetic. Consequently, Harryhausen may also be viewed as 'an agent who foregrounds the relationship between, and the material conditions of, art and commerce as the underpinning imperative of the approach'. Effectively, Harryhausen's animation is the primary determinant of the narrative and its outcomes, foregrounding the 'material conditions' of the film by invariably prompting the question of how his effects were achieved, and what might be lost by their absence: in the case of Harryhausen's films, virtually everything of narrative and symbolic consequence. Although the films in which Harryhausen participated – with a few exceptions – were essentially 'B' movies and cheaply made 'double bill' fare, these 'commercial' determinants have been relegated in recent years to less significant factors than the achievements of his art, and its distinctive aesthetic claims within the field of animation; his influence now evidenced and acknowledged in films as varied as Barry Purves' *Screenplay* (1992), Eric Fogel's *Celebrity Death Match* series, and Henry Selick's *Nightmare Before Christmas* (1993).

Harryhausen's auteurist claims begin early in his working life. His arts training at the Los Angeles City College and USC was comprehensive, engaging in fine arts, performance, and photography, and rooted him in a crafts orientation that in itself embraced the range of roles and functions that occur within film-making practice. Harryhausen's 'multi-skilling' was further enhanced during the war when he worked with director Frank Capra in the Special Services Division and contributed to the SNAFU cartoons, before collaborating with O'Brien again on *Mighty Joe Young* (1945), and undertaking the majority of the animation. His move into the 'B' movie arena, thereafter, was partly predicated on the industry viewing the stop-motion process as too expensive, and not seeing its potential, but producer, Charles Schneer recognised that Harryhausen's technique had a distinctive *cinematic* quality that would enhance films that some would describe as part of a 'trash' or 'lowbrow' aesthetic, or worse, 'low-budget exploitation'. Schneer valued 'B' movie culture, however, because it gave the creative personnel full artistic control, and was clear in its commercial imperatives; in this case, seeking out the 5–19-year-old demographic with the sales gimmick of calling Harryhausen's stop-motion animation within a live-action context 'Dynamation' based on the Buick campaign claiming 'Dynaflow' in the aerodynamics of the car. Harryhausen's first ventures, in *The Beast from 20,000 Fathoms* and *It Came from Beneath the Sea* (1953), were soon followed by the first 'Dynamation' feature, *The 7th Voyage of Sinbad* (1958). Schneer was also aware that he needed to change the public perception of animation as merely 'the animated cartoon', and further needed to promote work which foregrounded its stop-motion technique as an alternative to the established 'Disney' style in the animated form.

Crucial here, though, is the view that Harryhausen's 'art' emerges from the distinctiveness of his craft, and that it is the craft which drives the narrative, thematic and visual imperatives of the narratives he is dealing with. None of the films Harryhausen was instrumental in creating were 'star' vehicles, nor did they enjoy the possibility of being sought after because of their directorial credit; still a luxury perhaps only enjoyed by Hitchcock at this time. The films were vehicles for the spectacle Harryhausen created, and such 'spectacle' becomes the authorial signature ultimately understood by early devotees. The standard question posed of such illusionism was 'How is it done?' and the consequence of answering the question resulted in the recognition and importance of Harryhausen's contribution. James Cameron, director of *The Terminator* (1984), whose final robotic incarnation is a tribute to Harryhausen's 'skeleton' in *7th Voyage*, suggests:

> Ray was the ultimate vertically-integrated creative entity. He would conceive of the characters; often, he would work out the story to allow these characters to come into being. Then he would draw them; he would sculpt them, and then he would bring them to life through the craft of stop-motion. When you are a stop-motion animator, you are taking the place of an entire film crew; you are single-handedly creating a movie. In a way, you are the most unsung

hero in Hollywood; but in another way you are the most pure auteur in Hollywood.[5]

The concentration on Harryhausen's visual styling, the primacy of his aesthetic, and the extraordinariness of his technique – as a proof of his auteurist vision – has effectively distracted from, discouraged, or displaced any engagement with his work at the level of 'meaning'. The key critical engagements have sought to trace his presiding role within a process where the director is normally elevated, the producer sometimes credited with crucial imputs, and even the screenwriter or cinematographer allowed proper authorial credit. The process of proper valorisation has necessitated that Harryhausen be recognised as an *animator*, and that the vocabulary and aesthetic distinctiveness of *stop-motion animation* be acknowledged as the primary language of the features he made, which included it as the engine of their story-telling, design, and *mise-en-scène*. Consequently, returning again to our taxonomy, Harryhausen has a mode of authorship which operates as 'a historically adaptable idea which offers a way of implying and understanding how a film should be received'. One of the most incisive interviews with Harryhausen, for example, finds Adrian Wootton establishing Harryhausen's working process in order to locate him within the parameters of a film-making practice that formally echoes the development of an animated film, but which in essence still operates as a 'live-action' feature. As Harryhausen notes:

> Most of our projects, being mainly a visual pantomime, usually started with the drawings ... We would have many so-called 'sweat-box sessions' with Charles [Schneer], the writer and myself, where we would pick the storyline to pieces and try to fill in any missing pieces. The writer then did a treatment or first draft based on many of the drawings and ideas that surfaced in the meetings ... the script is finally completed, I then make about 350–400 simple pen-and-ink sketches of each cut in the effects sequences. They are simple sketches of each set-up ... The shooting of them has to be synchronised for the make-up of the shooting and production schedule ... our films were not what you would call a director's picture in the European sense of the word. With some directors, I had friction because they thought I was stepping on their toes when I directed the parts of my scenes ... I am the one who has to finally put all the pieces together. (quoted in Wootton 1996: 53–6)

This provides a significant insight into the working process, and points up two key aspects of Harryhausen's status as auteur. First, his process work chimes readily with the development of animated sequences as the principle aspects of the storyline *and* the technical imperatives of the final outcome. Second, his recognition that this was not a process which could offer the nominal directors of the films an 'orthodox' status as the recognised creator of the film, ironically reinforces his own credentials in the revision of the definition of the American auteur created in the likeness of the 'European' art-house and independent film-maker. Harryhausen implicitly suggests that he is the creative centre in the films he made, and that the principles of film-making *necessitated* by the process of animation, almost relegated the live-action context he worked within to second unit status. This elevates Harryhausen above the normal rigours of live-action film-making, and out of the ghetto of an effects tradition that often refuses to acknowledge the primacy of animation as a form at its heart; a situation echoed in contemporary 'blockbuster' film-making where much of the huge spectacle is in some way facilitated by the traditional, and more progressive, applications in animation.

The following interview with Harryhausen seeks to chart aspects of his career, and reinforce some of these observations.[6]

PW: *What was the major inspiration for becoming an animator?*

RH: The great original film that inspired my work was *King Kong*. When I saw the film I just could not believe that you could put such things on the screen. I was 13 at the time. I knew it was about a giant gorilla, but I could not figure out how it was done. I knew it wasn't a man in a suit, so I started to delve into the glories of stop-motion animation, and found out the technical ways in which it was created. That was some years later, of course, but it shows what one film can do – it was a complete inspiration. I just felt that this was what I wanted to do. I prepared myself over the years with the different crafts that it takes to create such images on the screen and it finally developed from a hobby into a profession.

PW: *What are the distinctive charcateristics of stop-motion animation?*

RH: To begin with, stop-motion animation was very similar to the animated cartoon. It was made one frame at a time. In the animated cartoon, you draw each frame with a slightly different, *progressive* movement of whatever you want the figure or object to do. Instead of using flat drawings, stop-motion animation uses a three-dimensional model, such as the one used in *King Kong*. The original 'King Kong' was about a foot tall, and was made up of metal ball and socket joints, so in whatever way you moved it, it would stay in that position. The model was covered with sponge rubber and bearhides. I believe it was actually rabbit fur that they used in film. Finally, after many hours of moving the model fractionally, and photographing that movement one frame at a time, it gives the appearance, when run at normal film speed, that the figure is moving.

PW: *King Kong still seems persuasive, even now. It is certainly a testimony to the modernity and innovation in the work of Willis O'Brien.*

RH: Willis O'Brien was the father of this type of animation in America. He first created three-dimensional model animation combined with human actors in *The Lost World*, but *King Kong*, of course, represented a great triumph in the process. O'Brien's technique was very complicated, especially in regard to the complexity of the shots in the sequence at the end where Kong scales the Empire State Building and is attacked by fighter planes. He had a skyline painted on a piece of glass, and behind it further pieces of glass with additional painted detail in order to get depth and perspective behind the model of the building. Fay Wray, the film's female star, was added to the scene by filming her on her own, and placing that footage into a space created by putting a piece of card on the model of the building to create 'a hole'. She was 'projected' into the space, and Kong was animated to properly interact with her. Then, of course, there were the miniature planes. For cutaways, they would use real planes, but when you see the long shots of the planes diving towards Kong, they use animated planes; each plane had to move frame by frame in order to synchronise with the movements of the gorilla. Such a complicated process becomes invisible if it is successful, and the whole thing looks simple. I loved the way that the film took you from a mundane world into a fantastic adventure, probably the most fantastic adventure seen on the screen up to that time. That was achieved mainly through stop-motion animation, and I think that accomplishment has been forgotten. The remake was an example of something which did not work because the fantasy element was left out to pursue the relationship between Kong and the girl. *King Kong* had a mysterious island with a dinosaur, prehistoric animals, wonderful jungles that you had never seen before outside of an engraving by Gustav Doré. Animation liberates the fantasy in the story.

PW: *Self-evidently, this was the kind of approach you wanted to bring to your own work.*

RH: I didn't analyse it to that degree until many years later, but in fact the whole approach did guide my thinking in the films I made later with Charles Schneer. I wanted to create fantasy never-never lands, and stop-motion was so much more valuable than other mediums. A way to explain how is to consider the relationship between the animated cartoon and live action. You have the problem that you are always aware that the animated cartoon is flat and the person is three-dimensional, even in something as well done as *Mary Poppins* [1967] or as sophisticated as *Who Framed Roger Rabbit*. But if you take films like *King Kong*, *The Lost World* or something like my own film, *Jason and the Argonauts*, you are not aware that there is a difference in what we might call 'texture'. A three-dimensional model is combined with a three-dimensional person, and it makes the idea of a fantasy film – something bigger than life, something completely unreal – somehow lifelike, and authentic. I think it is also a matter of tone. Again, the re-make of Kong was about wise-cracks between a girl and a dumb animal; you knew it was a guy in a gorilla suit and big models of large-scale hands. It did not have the integrity, or that innocent quality which is very difficult to achieve today.

PW: *Do you feel that stop-motion animation offers a unique visual aesthetic?*

RH: Every child is aware of a man in a suit. The *Godzilla* movies that were made in Japan, taking their influence from *The Beast From 20,000 Fathoms*, tried to simplify the process by simply putting a man in a rubber suit and shooting him at high speed stomping through a miniature set. There is a mysterious quality in animation that is perfect for fantasy films because it creates the illusion of a dream. The original *King Kong* had shifting hair, that some critics noticed and objected to, but I think it gave Kong a dream-like quality that it is not possible to achieve any other way. Using the technique was also a reaction to a particular period in Hollywood, where they started to try and do everything in a realistic manner. Film-making is theatre combined with the unique elements of cinema; animated film-making takes that idea one stage further. Even those wonderful Bette Davis movies were well conceived melodramas; they were not realistic, but even in those films, they did not really exploit the potential of the medium. Film is particularly appropriate to fantasy, a larger-than-life concept that you could not possibly photograph in the conventional way. Stop-motion fulfils that idea, and has a distinctive quality that is difficult to describe, but obvious to see.

PW: *That 'fantasy' aspect still seems to find its greatest expression in the creation of dinosaurs. Jurassic Park, Walking with Dinosaurs [1999], and Dinosaur all explore different avenues of narrative invention and technical innovation.*

RH: I was particularly impressed with *Jurassic Park*, basically because I was prepared to dislike it as so much of it was computer -generated. I was astounded by the results, though, especially in regard to those vast vistas and the herds of running animals, which would be very hard to achieve in stop-motion animation. I made a prehistoric dinosaur in *The Valley of Gwangi* [1968], which I took the trouble to be as authentic as possible because young children go to museums and are very knowledgeable about dinosaurs. I had a five-year-old tell me that I didn't know anything about Pterodactyls, because they do not have bat wings. He was right. I put bat wings on my Pterodactyls to give the illusion that they were airborne;a normal Pterodactyl has wings which do not give the impression that they can fly. These are the liberties you can take in animation. Ironically, many of the techniques used in stop-motion animation are part of the process in preparing CGI work, so traditional approaches are not entirely lost. The computer is another tool, and it all depends on what subject matter you are dealing with. Stop-motion or traditional cartoon-making are still very appropriate depending on what story you want to tell. The most important thing is that these approaches are not seen as things in themselves; you should not want to go to a film just to see the 'special effects'. They should be part of the whole story; the whole picture of the film. Many times in the early days we were accused of doing special effects for the sake of special effects, but actually, we chose the types of stories – Greek myths, for example – where you had to use every trick that you could possibly conceive in order to render the mythological concept on the screen. Very few films were made dealing with Greek myths, and when the Italians made those toga and sandals movies they were vehicles for muscle men. Even the 'Sinbad' movies made in Hollywood turned out to be romps over the sand dunes in baggy pants, so I wanted to take these subjects and treat them a little more seriously within their own fantasy context. I wanted to tell the stories of the Arabian Nights as a child might see and imagine them. I wanted to see a 'Cyclops' on screen. I wanted to develop a technique which would put these fairytales on screen in a way that suited them.

PW: *How did you try to achieve this, for example, in The 7th Voyage of Sinbad?*

RH: In *The 7th Voyage of Sinbad* I was trying to get away from the 'monster-on-the-loose' cycle that I had been involved with up until then. I destroyed Coney Island, I destroyed San Francisco, and I didn't want to keep doing that, especially as I thought that the original spirit and 'feel' of *King Kong* and *The Lost World* were increasingly lost. I was looking for a new outlet, and chose to work on a 'skeleton' sequence for the start of the film. I did eight big drawings showing the highlights of a proposed duel between an animated skeleton and a human in the 'Arabian Nights' style, drew up a twenty-page outline, and sought to pedle it in Hollywood. Nobody was interested, but I showed them to Charles Schneer, who I worked with before, and he persuaded Columbia to back us to make the film. Actually, those inspirational drawings are quite important. I once did a drawing for *One Million Years BC* [1966], where a Pterodactyl is picking up Raquel Welch, and it served to demonstrate the potential of the film to the backers before the picture was financed. It showed potential backers exactly what we intended to put on the screen, so these drawings had to be made keeping in mind that they had to be executed, so you could not draw any whimsical thing that came into your head. You had to be practical. In the film itself, we had a miniature model of Miss Welch, three inches high, and at the appropriate moment in the scene the Pterodactyl swooped to pick up the substituted model. Of course, the basic principle thatman lived in the days of the dinosaur has been violated many times. If cave people looked like Raquel Welch, then we've regressed over the years!

PW: *How was the skeleton sequence in The 7th Voyage actually executed?*

RH: The skeleton sequence became a prime exciting point which we felt we needed to have for a climax, and it was done in a very complicated way. We rehearsed many times on the set with a stuntman, Enzo Musumeci-Greco, who portrayed the skeleton. He was a very experienced swordsman and he went through the routine to get the actor used to the movements. Then we would photograph a piece of film featuring Kerwin Mathews, the star of the picture, 'shadow-boxing', and by that time he knew where to stop his sword where the provisional movements had been plotted. This piece of film I then combined with the miniature animated skeleton through the process of miniature projection. We photographed the person first, and projected the film on a small screen behind a small set featuring the miniature skeleton, ensuring that 'Sinbad' was the same size as the skeleton – effectively making the skeleton human-size in the frame – and then re-photographed that, frame-by-frame, through the whole process of the sword fight. One of the challenges of doing a skeleton is trying to hide the metal ball and socket armatures inside the figure because you are basically putting a skeleton on top of a skeleton. Each element of the skeleton is jointed, and each part must be moved in each frame. You have to keep all the movements synchronised, in order to give the illusion that the skeleton is a real living person.

PW: *You took that process to new heights, though, in Jason and the Argonauts.*

RH: The challenge in *Jason and the Argonauts* was having seven skeletons fighting three men which, of course, made it even more complicated. I would only average 13 to 15 frames a day, which is very little footage for a film of this nature. Of course, the accountants got irritated because time is money, and 15 frames is less than a foot of film. It actually took four-and-a-half months to do the *Jason* fight; two months to do the *7th Voyage*, so it is a time-consuming and expensive process.

PW: *The main pre-occupations of many discussions with you inevitably focus on your technique, and the distinctiveness of its achievement, but were you trying to explore any specific kinds of issue or theme?*

RH: *The Beast from 20,000 Fathoms*, of course, was based on the fear of what the atomic bomb would do. Similarly, *It Came from Beneath the Sea*. At the time we based our stories on the newspaper reports, and tried to elaborate on them in order to imagine a subject for a film which would reflect how much people were worried about the results of the atomic bomb. *Beast* was based on that, and the atomic bomb was blown up at the North Pole, so that the scene was at a far distance, but the consequences were clear. The beast was frozen in the ice, and became a figure to represent the spreading menace of radiation. The 1950s was a worrying time, and even in a movie like *Earth vs The Flying Saucers* (1952), we were dealing with the fears of invasion from outer space because at the time there were many so-called sightings of unidentified flying saucers, and unusual incidents. We wanted to make something pertinent to the period. Really, the transition from this kind of film came in the 1960s, when we tried to move from films that were about the fear of the unknown, particularly the unknown possibilities of what the atomic bomb might bring into our lives, through to something more escapist which used the unknown in the spirit of adventure and entertainment rather than anxiety.

PW: *Do you think that the spirit of exploring the 'unknown' has merely been overtaken by the idea of producing 'spectacle' for its own sake?*

RH: There has been a lot of recent debate about effects for the sake of effects. Hollywood even specialises in saying in publicity that such and such a picture has so many special effects in it. I still do not think that is what people particularly go to the cinema for. The special effects should be part of the story; you do not go to see a series of explosions or gruesome things for their own sake. Ironically, I think some of the more experimental or incoherent types of stories in the 1960s and 1970s might be responsible for this. Then 'disconnected incidents' had some sort of relationship for people trying to explore the medium, but now they are just disconnected incidents. There is no story to tell. There are no 'attractions', just happenings. I did not mind people not knowing who did the animation, because I wanted people to see special effects as a means of telling unusual types of stories. It is a pity that many special effects are used to glorify such negative subjects. We are often bombarded by negative things – people blown to pieces; heads dissolving with the eyes coming out – all these things pursue shock value, but irrational shock value, not working as part of sound storytelling dealing with inspirational, uplifting things. Animation still has a kind of innocence which can correct that.

PW: *In some ways you argue for your own 'invisibility' within the SFX tradition, but you were clearly the creative inspiration for, and maker of, your films. In recent years, many key figures including Phil Tippett, Dennis Muren and Henry Selick, as well as the academic and critical community have accorded you proper status as the significant auteur of the movies.*

RH: Basically, in the early days, I had to do everything myself. I've learned how to cast, how to make moulds et cetera, because I couldn't find anybody else to do it. I had to learn photography, and I had to take drama lessons to learn about performance. At one time I thought that

I wanted to be an actor, and I value the experience I had because I could act through the models. This was extremely valuable in the latter part of my career. In all the films except *Clash of the Titans,* I enhanced my technique in moving the models, and learned the way to concentrate to ensure the continuity of the action. Even in that film, though, there was Madam Medusa, which was a very complicated animated model. She had metal ball and socket joints inside her body which was cast in rubber. She had a suit, a bow and arrow, snakes on her arms and head, and a rattle in her tail, and could even breathe. Each snake on her head and arms had to have about eight joints in it, so in every frame of the film you had to move the tail of the snake, the head of the snake, and any intermediate position, plus all of her facial and hand gestures, so there were thousands of movements to create the image. Calibus, the creature with one cloven hoof, was also a very interesting project, because I had to combine model work with a live actor, so that the movement of each would be indistinguishable from the other. Such detailed work could only be done by one person. I always liked to work alone. I am always amused by so many of the modern films where you see a list of a hundred or so people involved in the special effects that I used to do all by myself. Of course, they are much more complicated today, but aside from that it was one man's interpretation of subject matter, and certainly not direction by committee. I would not get much joy out of sitting and pushing buttons in order to create an image. The joy comes in knowing different techniques and bringing them together to create that final image on the screen. I had a great deal of joy in the process of making stop-motion animated films.

Caroline Leaf

If Walt Disney may be viewed as a 'supra-auteur' by virtue of his overall position and affect in relation to his own studio, and Ray Harryhausen may be seen as an 'intra-auteur' by in effect authoring a text from within its ostensible live-action boundaries, then Caroline Leaf may be viewed in what is ironically a more traditional light, as an avant-garde, experimental film-maker, working largely independently, and with a more specifically self-conscious auteurist perspective.

Leaf made *Peter and the Wolf* (1968) using the technique of manipulating sand on a glass plate lit from beneath. Immediately, the innovatory aspect of the approach, and the 'hands-on' application of a single film-maker are self-evident, and point up authorial credentials that are more in line with the idea of 'a person who prompts and executes the core themes, techniques and expressive agendas of a film', and further, 'a figure around whom the key enunciative techniques and meanings of a film accrue and find implied cohesion'. This becomes clearer as she proceeds with her second film, *Orpheus* (1971), and ultimately, rescinds her authorship of her third film, *How the Beaver Stole Fire* (1971), because she could not edit the soundtrack. This is an important indicator of the desire to exercise complete control over all aspects of the film, and differs from the Disney version of this compulsion by being absolutely related to her own *crafting* of the film, and not merely her ownership.

Significantly, she was offered a context within which she had full creative control when she moved to the state-funded National Film Board of Canada who, while providing funding, a working context, and guidelines about the indigenous aspects of the Board's work, operate a non-interventionary policy on artists' films. Crucially, the Board promotes the value of 'art' through animation and is less concerned with commercial imperatives, and therefore may be viewed as a context in which the auteur operates as a maintenance of the ideology of the 'freedom of the artist', with all its implied benefits. Leaf's first Film Board film was another sand on glass piece, based on an Inuit legend called *The Owl Who Married A Goose* (1974). Her most renown and complex works, *The Street* (1976), *The Metamorphosis of Mr Samsa* (1977) and *Interview* (1979) followed, and consolidated her place as one of the acknowledged 'masters' of animation (see Halas 1987).

Leaf worked in other aspects of film-practice and theatre, producing, directing, writing and editing, before returning to animation in an advertisement for Saatchi and Saatchi called 'Paradise Found' (1988), and arguably her masterpiece, *The Two Sisters* (1990). The 1990s saw further work in advertising and fine art. The Council of the Zagreb World Festival of Animated Films bequeathed its Lifetime Achievement Award upon her in 1996, following on from figures like Norman McLaren, Chuck Jones, John Halas, Bob Godfrey and Dusan Vukotic.

Historian John Canemaker has suggested that Leaf's work recalls 'the pioneering works of J. S. Blackton and Emile Cohl' in their under-the-camera technique and mastery of 'metamorphosis', while also having the 'perfect sense of timing and implimentation of personality to individaute her characters [which] echoes the balletic movements and emotional impact of the best of Walt Disney'.[7] This combination of innovation and artistic sophistication marks out Leaf's auteurist claims in the sense that she delineates the specificities of her technique as new ways of working in the form in order to facilitate the greatest quality in their potential outcomes. Leaf enhances the 'form' to enable her to personalise and advance 'meaning', ensuring that both aspects are endemic to her as an individual artist. In this sense Leaf may be viewed as 'the embodiment and epitome of independent, original and potentially subversive vision in art, in support of the 'genius' myth', with some degree of legitimacy in the later claim given the distinctiveness of her work, and 'as a challenger to corporate, institutional and systemic oppression and coercion' by retaining her signature style and vision over a lifetime's work. Kit Laybourne notes that the story and choreographic elements are 'more generic to the personal style of Ms Leaf than they are to the technique of painting on glass', and adds 'a good measure of the artistry of *The Street* resides in the way that dialogue and sound effects are used as primary sources for constructing images and guiding transformations', before suggesting:

> It is astounding to most people that she animates all 'camera moves' (as they would be called in live-action film-making). A zoom, for example, is accomplished through manipulations in the artwork rather than by actually moving the animation camera. As a result the movement within the frame is free in the way that could never be accomplished through real camera moves. In Leaf's work the viewer's point of view is totally fluid. (Laybourne 1979: 99)

The modification of 'technique' enhances the very medium of animation while revealing its intrinsic qualities, and provides the aesthetic context in which Leaf's narrative and thematic concerns may be created and interpreted. In absolutely verifiable terms Leaf becomes an auteur 'who provides the organising principles of textual practices to engage with, and create, motivated spectatorial positions', while also being 'a person who offers direct statements and explanations about the artistic and thematic intentions of a film, within an evolving 'narrative' about the film-maker from work to work, which constitutes a personal vision', which is evidenced in the following interview.[8]

PW: *How did you get into animation as a field of work in the first instance?*

CL: I was a student at Harvard and took an animation class, which some thirty years later I have returned to teach. What I liked about animation

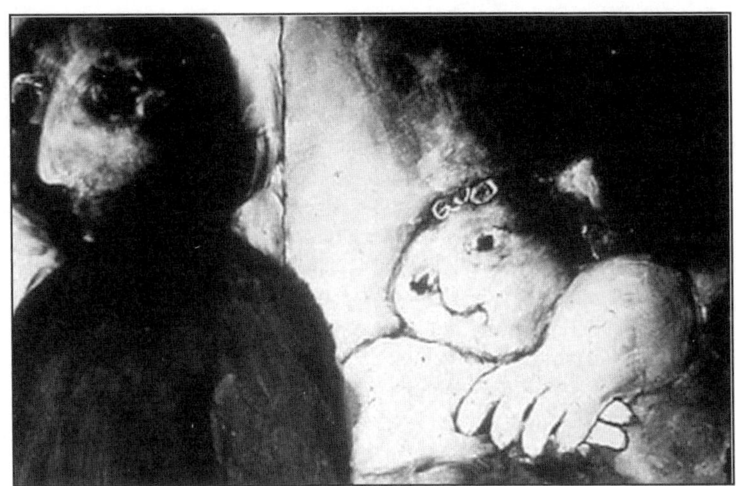

FIGURE 8 *The Street*

was that it gave me total control over what I was doing. In my animation class, everyone was working under the camera. The usual process for animation is to create artwork and then shoot it, and there are lots of possibilities to make tests and try things out to see if it is working, but when you are working under the camera, you are drawing and filming at the same time, and when you are finished there is nothing left but the film itself. So, I got used to working in that style, mainly because I wanted the process of 'drawing', but I couldn't draw with a pencil and paper, because that seemed such a commitment. So I dumped some sand out on to the light box, where I was working – there were a lot of beaches near Boston, near where I was at school, and I spent a lot of time on beaches – so that's how it began. My first films were made in this way. Sand that sits on a light box gets very warm and during the cold winter it was a very nice material to be handling. I like using my hands; I like having control and they're my best tools. Sand is a very sensuous medium. It has a great texture, and you can express emotion in it. I use my fingers and a pipe cleaner. The pipe cleaner is to make lines within shapes. For *Peter and the Wolf* I was just concerned with the black and white shapes in silhouette, but by the time I made the Kafka film – *The Metamorphosis of Mr Samsa* – I started to play with the density of the sand, and the perception of translucent material. I pressed a lot of objects into the sand to create various suggestive textures to represent a range of emotions.

PW: *You once described animation as a very 'intense' medium. Why do you find it appealing as a storytelling process?*

CL: It takes a lot of concentration to do it, because working under the camera is a particular kind of performance, and if you 'slip and fall' you just have to live with it. I was never influenced by cartoons, or other films really. I was more affected by painting and literature. The problem with literature is the words! For a literary idea to become a film it may go through many years of metamorphosis. I usually look for something that grabs me and inspires me visually. As I'm making the film, I try to leave behind the work of literature, and translate the words into images. I had friends who were animating, particularly at the National Film Board of Canada, and we were working in similar ways, and enjoyed each other's opinions of our work. I realised that storytelling, for me, is a form of restriction that is placed on me; that I have to fill out a story visually in relation to a basic story-line and I don't think I'd be creative if it wasn't for that kind of structuring restriction. Animation offers me that.

PW: *How did The Owl Who Married a Goose evolve?*

CL: This was the first film that I made when I moved up to Montreal. I had been working in Boston for a while as a freelancer, but I found it hard to do everything by myself, so I approached the National Film Board of Canada, which was a large, federally funded film production unit, and there were a lot of animators there, so I thought I would find a community I could work in. I went up there with my first film, and that's what won me a place there, although I had to wait nearly two years to begin. They were making a series of short films based on the legends of 'eskimo' people as they were then called.

PW: *You are a film-maker who has a very individual imprimatur on her work. How difficult was it to work in collaboration with other collaborators?*

CL: It is interesting that you should have that perception. Actually, I was given the film to make because the Film Board felt it suited the style I worked in. The Film Board wanted the *appearance* of working with native peoples – I know that doesn't sound very nice – but, they sent me up to the Arctic, and I studied carefully the work of the Inuit artists, to see if there was art which echoed the style I have of using large solid areas, and dark and light. I studied prints, and luckily it wasn't hard to find artists working in that way, so I chose the one I liked best, and she was working out in the western Arctic, and I went to work with her. Unfortunately, she was using tiny dots, having left her style of flat colours behind sometime before. In fact I could have made the film on my own as I ended up directing her and it was embarrassing, but I did learn up there that old women had been used by their fathers to go out hunting on the land, and to make the sounds of animals, and so after I had finished animating the film in Montreal, the next Spring I went up to the Arctic again to record the old women making the animal sounds, so probably the soundtrack would not have been so authentic if I hadn't done that. The Inuit people think it is very funny that this owl perished because he wasn't doing what he was supposed to do!

PW: *You would certainly have a clear claim to be one of the most auteurist of animated film-makers. Did you feel in any way constrained by National Film Board of Canada policy?*

CL: No. In the beginning, mainly because I had come from America, they wanted me to create Canadian content, but actually it was a good marriage. I was enabled to do what I wanted to do. I picked up on any creative opportunities that I thought I could do, and which suited my interests, and that led to making *The Street.* This was the first film that I made drawing people. I had been too shy to draw human figures. It felt presumptuous to me at that time as I had been working with fairly abstractly designed animal figures. I didn't study animals, and I didn't do any line-testing because of my technique, but I always felt that if I could imagine the movement then I could play it out in small increments frame by frame. I now had to do this with humans. I also wanted to work in colour and this film afforded me that possibility. This is what I wanted to experiment with, and I heard that the Board wanted to make a series of short films featuring the work of Canadian authors. Canada has wonderful literature; the country has supported its authors. I chose a story by Mordecai Richler, partly because it was written in my neighbourhood. *The Street* was actually one street away from where I was living, and I enjoyed the fact that I could do research by just looking around me. Richler, of course, was alive and well, and I felt that to respect a living author I had to take all of his text and turn it into a film. It was a slow process to learn that I really needed to drop as much of the original text as possible and turn the narrative into imagery. I then started to change the story around to make it work. Though it's based on his short story, it now has a different feeling; I think it has my own feeling now.

PW: *The Street is a very affecting film. I think it is particularly persuasive in its ink-on-glass technique, which enables extraordinary metamorphoses and shifts of perspective.*

CL: I made all the moves because I didn't want to make a cut. Another aspect was that I could not generate enough material to experiment with editing. Because I was working with a medium that smudged and smeared and disappeared, and I wanted to move from one place to another in the narrative as quickly as possible and without fuss, I found that 'rubbing out' the ink was the best way, adding the next image straight away. I did that as an intuitive process rather than with the aid of pre-storyboarding. I like making movement itself, and for example, in the last panaramic shift in the film, I just wanted to show what it was like for me to look out from my window across the space. Ironically, the film was put on the shelf for a while because it wasn't considered polite to show children talking about their grandparents dying, and it took a number of years for that attitude to change. Then it became a useful teaching tool to address how kids talk about their grandparents dying! I really dislike fairytales, and I didn't want this to be like one. I wanted an approach to animation that would express what I wanted to say. I like dealing with emotions and relationships, and I think this kind of animation can deal with that. I like stories in enclosed spaces. I read stories about the Canadian Prairies but I just didn't know what to do with wide-open spaces. Something about the enclosed, local, interior aspects of the story were very appealing.

PW: *The Metamorphosis of Mr Samsa, your adaptation of Kafka's 'The Metamorphosis' seems especially suited to your approach – especially the elliptical way of approaching narrative – and your emerging concerns.*

CL: It was made at the same time as *The Street* and was made over a period of years, because I actually started it before I left Boston. I liked the Kafka story for its themes, particularly the issue about 'appearance', and the idea that the interior state may be very different from what you see on the outside, which in this instance is a very tragic circumstance to be in. I liked the movement from the humane to the monstrous, and I liked the idea of 'metamorphosis', but narrative was my preoccupation. I felt that I was in some ways limited because in the novel there was so much more about the tension between the human and the consciousness of the beetle that I didn't get because I wasn't using language. On the other hand, the use of animation meant I could suggest other things, though, and the most important thing became the expression of 'feeling' through story, and ultimately, how the film looks to achieve that. When I'm actually animating it becomes a visual problem frame by frame, and I almost forget what the narrative is about, yet at the same time I can say that I keep quite strictly to an overall narrative line – a controlling idea – that I have set myself to explore. I try not to vary too much because sometimes an image looks interesting in itself, and I want to pull it this way and that, but I prevent myself because the character as I have expressed it visually might break down. I'd like an audience to be touched, to have sympathy and identification, and I try not to distract myself by being too self-conscious about having a point of view, and rather to create emotion through imagery.

PW: *Interview, your next film, is a departure in the sense that it is informed by many styles and approaches. It is also a much more overtly personal film. This was clearly something different. How was the film received?*

CL: It was a different kind of film because I was co-directing with Veronica Soul, who works in a different style than I do. The idea came from murmurings in the corridors at the Film Board that there was going to be a series of films about the animation directors at the unit. I thought it would be fun to do one about ourselves. We interviewed each other extensively – that's why it's called *Interview* – and then we selected different parts to animate. We then came together to edit the film. I think this film has had a different audience with a different level of appreciation. Women have enjoyed looking at this film. I look at the film now and I wonder why we included certain things that we did. There was a lot of nonsense there. I think we were just having fun. There wasn't much planning but we were seeking to say a certain amount about our working habits. We thought that everything about living related to work, so we included a very broad range of things as the subject matter of the film. Really I was blinded by the revelations of my own shyness and awkwardness, and this is what makes me feel uncomfortable seeing it with an audience, and though some have argued that there is a sexual connotation to the relationship in the film, this is really us just playing with the audience!

PW: *Within the film we get a glimpse of your 'ink-on-glass' technique. You seemed to be planning the film with small drawings. How were you developing technically?*

CL: My early films were not storyboarded and the sound was done afterwards. *The Street* wasn't ever storyboarded from beginning to end, but the soundtrack was done beforehand, and it meant I could alter the timing of certain things. I actually started animating that in different places in the narrative, and worked outwards until the story connected up. I listen a lot to the sound because it gives me indications for lip-synching, but more for engaging with physical gesture and the body language of the characters. I directed the sound after I'd done enough drawings to know how I would direct it, what kind of people the characters were, and what I wanted to do with them. Later films had more storyboarding but it's always about sound and image working together. Usually, as I am working, sound ideas come to me. I work better with sound effects than music, so the elements of 'quiet' become important. I do not necessarily storyboard the film at the beginning but I always did some drawings on the animation table before I started animating a scene so I knew where I was going to and wouldn't get lost. *Interview* was interesting for me because this was the first time that I wasn't taking somebody else's story. I was making my own story with Veronica. I was excited working with her, especially for the editing, because the 'chunks' that fit together could have gone in any kind of order. It didn't save time, though; we talked too much! It is history now, but it is still 'me', and at the time I felt that the openness was a way to touch people.

PW: *Interview was made in 1979, and you didn't return to animation until 1990. What happened in the intervening period, and what brought you back to make The Two Sisters?*

CL: As in *Interview*, in *Two Sisters* I complain a lot about being stuck in a dark room. After *Interview* I left the dark room and I had grand ideas about what I would do as a scriptwriter, as a live-action film-maker, and I tried all those things but I inched my way back to animation because I wanted to have total control. The live-action films I was happiest directing during this period involved full-scale puppets – basically people in costumes – working against painted or projected backgrounds. Budget constraints meant it was a much more uncomfortable shoot. It was chaotic and disorganised. I couldn't get the sense of movement through space that I could achieve in animation. One story which I had been working on over many years, which at one point became an hour-long fiction film, was not going to work, and I didn't want to make it, so I took some themes from it and reduced it down to an animated film project. It had a tortuous route to completion over eight or nine years, and it started from my love of Bulgakov's novel

'The Master and Marguerita', of which there are only remnants in the film; the main one being the image of the outsider who comes into a very stable but not very healthy situation, and upsets the equilibrium, the status quo, and he does it for morally good reasons, and there is that character in the film. He has two-coloured eyes which I think Oland in the novel has, but that is about [all] that's left. When I knew I wanted to do an animated film I reduced the enormous scope of the novel down to a study of the power relationships between three people. I love colour, but I kind of evolved what is basically a two-tone system of animation.

PW: *In this film you use another technique, and use design to an important symbolic effect.*

CL: When I came back to animation I still didn't want to be in the dark room, and I decided that if I scratched the film emulsion, then there is no camera, and I could do it anywhere. Film has a celluliod base; exposed film is black and it has layers of colour in it which you could scrape and get through to the white. You could work through the layers of colour for different effects. It was a complicated story and I needed lots of detail so I used the larger-scale 70mm IMAX format to get more in the frame. At first I had the gaoler sister and the victim sister and it seemed boring to me until I realised that they both wanted the situation to remain the same because they were both needing and getting something from it. The sister who writes needs to be protected, and the sister who looks after her, needs to feel needed and loved. With that dynamic I felt I had the story base which the outsider breaks into. The victim sister becomes uglier and uglier; as I worked on her she became more monstrous. I had to have someone who wanted to hide herself because she was deformed, so I had her mouth distorted – the original title of the film was 'Burnt Mouth' – but I wanted to keep her big expressive eyes. I wanted her to be sympathetic but at the same time be grotesque, and I think animation is the perfect vehicle to achieve that. I had some difficulty with the outsider figure, who is in some ways simplistic because he swims across some water, and turns their lives around by letting the victim sister into the sunlight. The balance between the symbolic storytelling – the light and the dark – and the realistic presence of the man who comes in is important, because I wanted to create empathy for them as real people, as well as producing 'the idea'. The more you feel for the sister, the more you might accept the symbolism; if I have succeeded this may work; otherwise the male figure could be laughable.

PW: *Looking back, how do you evaluate your own work?*

CL: I recently went back to Harvard to teach the class I took, and I needed to be more critical and analytical of my own work, and more self-conscious about what was important to me and what I value, and what it came down to was not technique, but a method of being creative, and helping people to express what they wanted to say. I haven't compared my work to other people's work. I know the outsider figure is a constant in my work. I think that's how I feel about myself, and my films express my feelings about that.

A brief conclusion

This engagement with the histories, processes, generic definitions and authorial issues in animation is designed to introduce a range of work, and prompt some discussion and debate about what is still an often marginalised and less regarded field of filmic and artistic practice, despite the form's omnipresence in contemporary visual cultures and cinema. It is a form which has produced great artists and artworks, and this is insufficiently acknowledged. It is my hope that this analysis achieves this, but more importantly, theorises areas which have been neglected, and which may provide the catalyst for minds greater than my own to explore and celebrate the form. This is not all folks...

APPENDIX

Given the thousands of animated films that have been made since the early years of cinema, the 'Animation Timeline' presented here is necessarily selective, but it seeks to introduce a variety of 'histories' of animation from a number of contexts and cultures. It attempts to provide an insight into a range of animated films, related events, and pertinent issues which will connect to this analysis of animation as a unique cinematic language, and the address of its subsequent relationship to two highly familiar and taken-for-granted aspects of film criticism: authorship and genre. It should be also be stressed that the 'Timeline' is provided to stimulate interest, and encourage readers to pursue certain films and engage in more research. In many senses animation, despite its longevity, popularity and scale of achievement, is still underwritten about, and further work is welcome.

As I was preparing the 'Timeline' it became increasingly difficult to select what should be included and what should be left out. No doubt, more invested readers will dispute some entries and hold their hands up in horror at particular omissions. My first advice is to read each entry fully as often an entry will include information about films earlier than the one named, and some concern later work. Overall, my criteria for inclusion is informal, partly based on renowned works which are addressed within extant animation literature, and partly on my own preferences and limited knowledge. The key issue, though, is that the 'Timeline' serves as a parallel model of information to accompany the discussion, and hopefully, will enable further work to take place in the classroom and facilitate social debates that may follow thereafter.

The 'Timeline' that follows, therefore, seeks to demonstrate the historical, technological and artistic development that the field of animation has achieved from the earliest experiments in developing motion pictures through to the state-of-the-art achievements and cultural presence of the form in the present day. It should be used as a range of examples which *define* a form, and illustrate it from a number of perspectives, operating as a reference point for the conceptual debates that may be drawn from it.

DATE	FILM	NOTABLE EVENT OR ISSUE
1798		Etinne Robertson creates the *Phantasmagoria*, a sophisticated 'magic lantern' to project images.
1830		Michael Faraday creates a revolving wheel to enhance visual illusions.
1833		Joseph Antoine Plateau consolidates his theories on the persistence of vision by making a *Phenakistascope*, in a which a revolving disk with images on it appeared to put those images in motion.
1834		William Horner creates the *Zoetrope*, a revolving drum with observation slits where the sequence of pictures inside appears to move when the cylinder is spun.
1839		Henry Langdon Childe enhances the magic lantern to incorporate

		dissolving images, and the first implications of one movement to another.
1853		Franz Von Uchatius creates the *Kinetiscope* which projects the illusion of motion in drawings.
1866		L.S.Beale devises the *Choreuscope* which enables a magic lantern slide to project moving drawings.
1870		Henry Heyl invents the *Phasmatrope* which projects moving photographic images, initially of a dancing couple.
1877		Emile Reynaud patents the *Praxinoscope* which uses mirrors within a spinning cylinder to create the illusion of moving images. He advances his work a year later with the Théâtre-Optique praxinoscope. By 1880 he had created a projection system.
1890		American print journalism embraced first cartoon strips, including Richard Outcault's 'Yellow Kid'.
1892		Reynaud projects the *Pantomimes Lumineuses*.
1895–1896		Robert Paul's *Theatograph*; Edison's *Vitascope*; the Skladanowsky's *Bioscop* and the Lumière's *Cinématographe* project moving film images.
1896		Georges Méliès uses stop-motion animation – the creation of movement frame-by-frame – as part of his repetoire of trick effects. Méliès was also a 'lightning cartoonist' who accelerated the movement of the drawings by manipulating camera speeds. In 1900 he made *le Livre Magique* where drawings appear to become human beings.
1897	*A Visit to the Spiritualist*	Vitagraph, co-founded by Albert E. Smith and J. Stuart Blackton use stop-motion animation.
	Humpty Dumpty Circus	A stop-motion animation using small jointed figures and moving objects.
1898	*The Cavalier's Dream*	The Edison Company patent a stop-motion animation in which an environment changes while a man is sleeping.
1899	*Matches: An Appeal*	Briton, Arthur Melbourne Cooper may lay claim to have made one of the first 3D animated advertisements. Critics have suggested that the film may have been made later, however.
1900	*The Enchanted Drawing*	Albert E. Smith and J. Stuart Blackton beccame increasingly sophisticated in noticing how the new film medium worked, and in consequence, creating effects, using stop motion to enhance 'Lightning cartooning' as it was executed in vaudeville routines. *The Enchanted Drawing* shows a man smiling while drinking and smoking.
1902	*A Trip to the Moon*	Méliès uses stop-motion animation as part of his armoury of fantasy effects.
	Fun in a Bakery Shop	Edwin S. Porter uses stop-motion animation to show loaves made from clay being sculpted into the faces of famous people.
1905	*Train Collision* *The Electric Hotel*	Spaniard Segundo de Chomón was one of the first film-makers to use models in animated shorts. He also worked with Italian film director, Giovanni Pastrone on a sequence in *The War and the Dream of Momi* (1916).
1906	*Humourous Phases of Funny Faces*	J. Stuart Blackton's important transitional film showing the ways animation could enhance the principles of the'lightning sketch'. Vitagraph's later film, *The Haunted Hotel* (1907), used stop-motion object animation, and established a market for this kind of distinctive film-making practice.
1908	*The Sculptor's Nightmare*	Billy Bitzer's stop-motion creation of busts of political figure heads laughing and smoking. The relationship between busts, statues and moving sculpture has a long tradition in animated films.

	Fantasmagorie	Frenchman Emile Cohl's ground-breaking film based on the surrealist principles of the *incoherent* artists.
1910		Arnaldo Ginna's technique of painting directly on to film was adopted by Len Lye and Norman McLaren much later. Ginna believed that colour and form could develop in the same way as musical notes and chords. He suggested that a 'chromatic motif' – the progression of colour combinations through an animated time sequence – was similar to a 'musical motif' which developed throughout a piece of music.
1911	*The Cameraman's Revenge*	Landislaw Starewich's 3D model animation using insects in a love-triangle story also makes self-reflexive comment on the voyeuristic aspects of cinema itself. Starewich was simultaneously commenting on the melodramatic aspects of American cinema, while consolidating the literariness of the scenario in the spirit suggesting by key figures in the development of the Soviet film industry. Starewich later made the influential *The Tale of the Fox* (1930) when he left Moscow for Paris. His 'Aesop'-like fables were fuelled with dark undercurrents and social satire. Producer Alexander Khanzhonkov discovered Starewich through a news story that he had won a Christmas costume competition for three consecutive years. Starewich came to Moscow, quickly becoming a versatile film-maker in a number of styles, influenced by the engraver, Grandville.
	Little Nemo in Slumberland	Winsor McCay and Walter Arthur produced a film called *Winsor McCay Makes His Cartoons Move* early in 1911 profiling McCay's technique of using rice paper cels. McCay's later film is about a little boy's surreal dreams based on his own *New York Times* comic strip.
1912	*The Story of a Mosquito*	Arguably, the first animated 'horror' film, featuring a vampiric mosquito, and consolidating McCay's technique drawn from his skills as a draughtsman and illustrator.
1913	*The Newlyweds*	Comic strip animations featured in Pathé newsreels. Eclair produced and Emile Cohl animated *The Newlyweds*, based on George McManus' comic strip.
		John R.Bray and Raoul Barré simultaneously evolve systematic quasi-industrial processes for the production of cartoons in a Fordist 'assembly line' manner.
1914	*The Dinosaur and the Missing Link*	Willis O'Brien produces a short, stop-motion animated film in anticipation of his later film *The Lost World* (1925), and his groundbreaking effects in *King Kong* (1933).
	Gertie the Dinosaur	Winsor McCay's celebrated dinosaur film, featuring Gertie, a creature like his mosquito, characterised by a full range of personality traits and gestures. McCay interacted with the film in his vaudeville routine. The film consolidated his technique of animating 'in-between' movement between two extreme poses of his creatures.
		J. R. Bray and Earl Hurd apply for patents on their 'cel animated' production process. Bray had produced *The Artist's Dream* (1913) as a pilot for a system that would become an industry standard.
1915	*Krazy Kat and The Katzenjammer Kids* *Farmer Al Falfa*	Gregory La Cava supervises cartoons based on the Hearst International comic strips, *Krazy Kat and The Katzenjammer Kids*. Paul Terry produces the first *Farmer Al Falfa* cartoon.
	The Animated Grouch Chasers	The Edison company releases Raoul Barré's *Grouch Chaser* cartoons. A year later, Barré joined with Charles Bowers to produce films, and to make Bud Fisher's *Mutt and Jeff* comic strip as a cartoon.
		The Fleischer Brothers experiment with the process of 'rotoscoping': animating over live-action footage.

1916		As part of an increasingly industrialised process in studios, new innovations occurred to speed and enhance the work. Bill Nolan, for example, creates a moving background beneath foreground cel animated figure action.
1917	*El Apóstol*	Argentinian Quirino Cristiani's hour-long myth about social redemption may be recognised as the world's first animated feature.
	Ever Been Had?	Dudley Buxton's British cartoon which self-reflexively shows a film within a film, anticipating the idea of the last man on earth after a wartime apocalypse. Buxton also worked with celebrated British animator Anson Dyer on *John Bull's Animated Sketchbook* (1920) and *Kiddigraphs*, featuring *Three Little Pigs* (1922) and *Little Red Riding Hood* (1922). Dyer also worked on what was going to be the feature length *The Story of the Flag* (1927), but this was released in six separate episodes.
	*The Naughty Mailbox** *The Lazy Sword*** *Imokawa Muzuko, the Concierge****	Seitaro Kitayama* Junichi Kouchi** and Oten Shimokawa*** are the pioneers of Japanese animation industry, all making films as early as 1917. The Japanese industry was later to create the internationally successful manga animé films, and a range of exportable indigenous and crossover films and TV series which proliferate to the present day.
		Viking Eggeling creates experimental abstract animation in the spirit of a modernist avant garde. Eggeling's most influential work was *The Diagnonal Symphony* (1922).
1918	*The Sinking of the Lusitania*	Winsor McCay makes what is arguably the first animated documentary, although this may have been preceded by a film made in Britain by about the same event, which has since been lost.
1919	*Feline Follies*	Pat Sullivan and Otto Messmer make the first Felix the Cat film. Messmer's authorship of the Felix films was not acknowledged, however, until long after.
	Out of the Inkwell: The Tantalising Fly	Max Fleischer introduces his part-animated, part-live-action series, featuring Koko the Clown.
		Richard Collard, known by his pseudonym, 'Lortac', established what may have been one of the first properly organised animation studios in France, servicing Eclair with animated inserts for newsreels.
1920	*Aesop's Fables*	Paul Terry introduces a series which was arguably influential on the Disney 'animal' universe. Initially distributed by RKO, Terry's films were then distributed in 1928, by the new Van Beuren studio, later satirised by animator and feature director, Frank Tashlin as the 'Van Boring' studio. Terry's *Dinnertime* (1928) may make claim to be the first sound cartoon advancing the Fleischer experiments, but falling short of the full sound synchronisation in *Steamboat Willie*.
1921	*Rhythmus 21* *Lichtspiel Opus 1*	Hans Richter completes his first abstract experimental work, *Rhythmus 21*, partly in collaboration with Eggeling. He makes two more variations on the *Rhythmus* film in the next four years. Oskar Fischinger also begins experimental work, animating the changes in the colours and shapes as he removed slices from a prepared wax cylinder. Fischinger also worked with cut-outs and silhouettes. Walter Ruttman released his first abstract animation, *Lichtspiel Opus 1*, which anticipated his *Opera* series in the following two years, before he assisted Lotte Reiniger on her *Prince Achmed* film.
	Laugh-O-Grams	Walt Disney's first cartoons – adaptations of fairytales including *Puss in Boots* and *The Four Musicians of Bremen* – actually feature Disney's own animation.
1922	*Colonel Heeza Liar*	John R. Bray released a series of cartoons featuring 'Colonel Heeza

		Liar', based on the exploits of President Teddy Roosevelt.
1923	*Einstein's Theory of Relativity*	The Fleischer Brothers make a ground-breaking four-reel educational film.
	The *Alice* Comedies	Walt Disney forms his own company, and reverses the Fleischer Brothers conceit in the *Out of the Inkwell* series, and puts the live-action figure of Alice in an animated environment. Some of these films were the last Disney himself animated, leaving this task to Ub Iwerks and Rollin Hamilton. The part-animated, part-live-action film has a rich tradition in animation and includes such notable work as *You Ought to Be in Pictures* (1940), featuring Porky Pig and Leon Schlesinger. *Space Jam* (1997) represents full integration of live action and cartoon characters within a 3D virtual environment.
1924	*Ballet Mécanique*	Painter Fernand Léger's influential avant-garde work including full animation, painting directly on to film, and Méliès-like special effects, as well as live action, was a direct statement about making art-works which foregrounded their own artifice and used objects as a challenge to the machine culture and consumerist ethic of the modern industrial environment.
	Soviet Toys	Animation played a small part in the illustration of political manifestos and in the advancement of radical film-making in the Soviet Union. Dziga Vertov used animated inserts in the *Kino-Pravda* newsreel, including *Soviet Toys*, by Ivanov and Buskin. Mikhail Tsekhanovsky's *Post* (1929), based on a children's story by Samuel Marshak and illustrator, Lebedev, was shown by American architect Frank Lloyd Wright to Walt Disney as a possible model for the development of animation. Tsekhanovsky also made *Pacific 231* (1930) but fiercely resisted American industrialisation techniques, preferring the distinctiveness of his drawn animation over the cel animated process. Working with Dmitre Shostakovich, Tsekhanovsky began a full-length animated comic opera, based on *The Tale of the Priest and his Servant, Blockhead*, a poem by Pushkin. The film was not completed but served to preserve indigenous approaches against Disney/Fleischer influences.
	The *Song Car-tunes*	The Fleischer Brothers made films related to popular songs, featuring a 'bouncing ball' device that moved along the lyrics while cinema audiences sang along to the piano accompaniment.
1926	*The Adventures of Prince Achmed*	Lotte Reiniger's lyrical, silhouette cut-out animation had a significantly different aesthetic from the emergent animated cartoon in the United States, and lasted some 65 minutes. Reiniger's work was profoundly influential on women animators seeking to use the form for individual aesthetic and social purposes.
1927	*The Whale*	Japanese animator Noburo Ofuji creates animation with the distinctive semi-transparent paper material, *chigoyami*, echoing Lotte Reiniger's cut out style.
	Oswald the Rabbit	Walt Disney introduces a 'character' series featuring Oswald, whose design anticipates the far more successful Mickey Mouse.
	The Octopus Bone	The prolific Japanese animator, Yasuji Murata, uses cel animation and creates a Disneyesque animal universe.
1928	*Eveready Harton in Buried Treasure*	The first pornographic cartoon, probably made in New York by a cross-studio ensemble of notables, who may have included Max Fleischer, Paul Terry and Walter Lantz. Possibly made for Winsor McCay's birthday party, or as a stag film.
	Plane Crazy *The Gallopin' Gaucho* *Steamboat Willie*	These Ub Iwerks-designed and animated shorts defined the Disney style and echoed contemporaneous events; *Plane Crazy*, Lindburgh's Atlantic crossing; *Gaucho*, the prominance of Valentino. *Steamboat Willie* remains a landmark in animation as the first fully-synchronised sound cartoon, and for the introduction

		of a mischievous Mickey Mouse.
1929	*Skeleton Dance*	Walt Disney's near-abstract dance animation, featuring a soundtrack by Carl Stalling, and anticipating Disney's gothic themes in many of his shorts and features.
		Paul Terry establishes 'Terrytoons', producing over 1000 cartoons by 1952.
1930	*Sinkin' in the Bathtub*	The first MGM 'Looney Tune' – an obvious parody of Disney's 'Silly Symphony' – featuring a black-faced child, Bosko, and produced by Hugh Harman and Rudolph Ising, whose names became fortuitously coupled in the 'Harman-Ising' cartoons.
	Dizzy Dishes	In one of its 'Talkartoons', Max Fleischer creates his first incarnation of 'Betty Boop', initially as a dog. She was later named 'Betty' in *Betty Co-Ed* (1931) and became Betty as we know her in *Any Rags* (1932).
	King of Jazz	Walter Lantz produces the first Technicolor cartoon sequence in a full-length live action colour feature.
1931	*Flip the Frog*	After leaving Walt Disney, Ub Iwerks produces his first, less than successful, character series, released through MGM.
	Lady Play Your Mandolin	The first 'Merrie Melodies' cartoon – again, another parody of the 'Silly Symphony' – and a further example of animation's intrinsic relationship to popular music. Many of these early animations from all the emergent studios may be viewed as the first 'pop videos'.
1932	*The Perimeters of Light and Sound and Their Possible Synchronisation*	Mary Ellen Bute and Leon Thurmin experiment with the concept of drawing with electronically determined codes; arguably, the first form of computer generated animation. Bute made *Rhythm in Light* (1934), *Synchromy No 2* (1935), *Escape* (1938) and *Tarantella* (1939) all illustrating pieces of classical music.
	Experiments in Hand Drawn Sound	Oskar Fischinger continues his experiments in 'visual music', culminating in the synchronisation of colours and forms to Nicolai's overture to 'The Merry Wives of Windsor' in *Composition in Blue* (1935), arguably the inspiration for Disney's *Fantasia* (1940), which Fischinger was temporarily involved in making before leaving feeling disillusioned with Disney's approach, and his claims to the authorship of individual artist's work.
	Flowers and Trees	Walt Disney orders an already three-quarters made black and white cartoon to be remade fully in Three-Strip Technicolor. It won the first Oscar for animated short films
1933	*Three Little Pigs*	Walt Disney's most fully formed 'personality' animation short, whose signature ditty, written by Frank Churchill, 'Who's Afraid of the Big Bad Wolf?' became a rallying cry against the damaging effects of the Depression.
	Betty Boop's Snow White	The Fleischer Brothers' surreal take on the Snow White fairytale, featuring Betty, Koko and Bimbo, as well as a rotoscoped performance from Cab Calloway singing 'St James' Infirmary Blues'. A *cartoon noir.* The Fleischer studios made a number of films featuring Betty which included transient imagery of her genitalia and breasts which eluded the censors.
	Popeye the Sailor	Max Fleischer introduces the popular blue collar sailor.
1934	*Honeymoon Hotel*	The first colour 'Merrie Melodies' cartoon.
	The Wise Little Hen	The first film featuring Donald Duck. Donald Duck became the Disney studio's most popular character and was used extensively in wartime propaganda shorts.
	Night on Bald Mountain	Alexander Alexeieff and Clare Parker create their first 'pin-screen' animation, utilising the lighting effects upon a thousand pin screen, where different levels of pins were raised to create an

		image, and photographed one frame at a time.
	Poor Cinderella	Max Fleischer first combines 3D sets with standard cel animation in his 'Color Classics' cartoons.
	L'Idee	Berthold Bartosch creates an atmospheric cut-out film based on Frans Masereel's wood-cuts. The film lasted 30 minutes and featured an electronic score by Arthur Honegger.
	The Discontented Canary	Hugh Harman and Rudolph Ising create the first 'Harman-Ising' cartoons for MGM called 'Happy Harmonies'.
1935	*A New Gulliver*	Alexander Ptushko's politicised puppet animation, made with moulded wax dolls, up-dates Swift's story seeing Gulliver as the champion of an oppressed proletariat and demonstrating the benefits of modernisation in the industrial landscape.
	The Band Concert	The first colour Mickey Mouse cartoon which may be viewed as a summation of Disney's stylistic combination of personality animation, situational story-telling and gag construction, and image/music synchronisation.
	A Colour Box	Len Lye's stylish and innovative abstract film, sponsored by the Post Office, and culminating in information about parcel post costs! Lye also completed a puppet film, *The Birth of a Robot* (1936) and *Rainbow Dance* (1936), featuring a human figure and varying colour combinations.
	I Haven't Got a Hat	The first cartoon featuring Porky Pig.
1936	*The Country Cousin*	Disney explores a town and country theme, comparing rural innocence with urban sophistication. Frank Tashlin argued that the mouse featured in the cartoon is a prototype for all cute mice in cartoons thereafter, particularly Jerry, in the Hanna Barbera *Tom and Jerry* series.
	Popeye the Sailor meets Sindbad the Sailor	The Fleischer Brothers produce the first extended-length cartoon short.
		The Van Beuren Studio closes.
1937	*Love on the Wing*	Norman McLaren's abstract film advertising air-mail is viewed as 'too Freudian' by a British government minister who saw sexual connotations in the imagery. McLaren becomes a key figure in the field creating numerous variations on the interface between animation and avant garde film-making practice. *Allegro* follows in 1939.
	Clock Cleaners	Ben Sharpsteen's Disney short combining a state-of-the-art understanding and enhancement of slapstick comic principles, and a comment upon the inability of traditional folk cultures to come to terms with late modernity and the consequences of the machine age.
	The Old Mill	Walt Disney inaugurates the first use of the multi-plane camera in a short animation, to create realistic perspective and movement through the depth of field.
	Porky's Duck Hunt	Daffy Duck makes his debut against what would become his long term adversary comic dupe
	Snow White and the Seven Dwarfs	First thought of as 'Disney's folly', the film which advanced the animation medium. The first full-length, sound-synchronised, Technicolor animated feature musical.
		A strike occurs at the Fleischer Brothers Studio, signaling the first full impact in the struggle for unionisation within the animation studios, a fate that was to befall the Disney Studio four years later.
1938	*Porky's Hare Hunt*	A prototypic 'Bugs Bunny' appears in this cartoon, but Frank Tashlin has argued that the real design basis for Bugs was in

		Disney's *The Tortoise and the Hare* (1935).
1939	*Gulliver's Travels*	The Fleischer Brothers' first full-length feature.
	Peace on Earth	Hugh Harman's part-Disneyesque 'cute', part-documentary 'real' evocation of the consequences of war. Nominated for an Oscar and the Nobel Peace Prize, and endorsed in many social contexts for its anti-war message.
	Pinocchio	Arguably, Disney's masterpiece. A gothic tour-de-force exploring the moral, social and material world, and illustrating the complex processes of redemption and fulfilment.
1940	*Puppetoons*	Paramount sign émigré George Pal to produce a series of 3D puppet animations using his 'replacement' technique of creating multiple different body parts as they move through a sequence, photographing each one frame at a time before it is 'replaced' by the next head, arm, leg et cetera. He was assisted by Ray Harryhausen, later creator of 'Dynamation' in a range of features.
		The Bauhaus influenced John Halas, and Joy Batchelor establish Halas and Batchelor Studios in England. The Larkins studio also opens, often anticipating UPA in its graphic style in educational films.
	The Wild Hare	Tex Avery creates Bugs Bunny, and his signature catchphrase, 'What's Up, Doc?'
	Princess Iron Fist	Disneyesque first feature for the Wan Brothers based at the Shanghai studios in China, preceded by the graphic intensity of the *Songs of the Anti-Japanese War* (1938), and ultimately followed by *Uproar in Heaven* (1965), based on the traditional Monkey stories, as an on-going attempt to create animated films with indigenous styles and stories. Xu Jingda's *Nezha Triumphs Over the Dragon King* (1979) and Hu Jinqing's *Snipe Clam Grapple* (1984) also reflect this.
	Puss Gets the Boot	Hanna Barbera create the first Tom and Jerry cartoon.
	Knock Knock	Walter Lantz introduces Woody Woodpecker.
1941	*Fantasia*	Walt Disney's controversial feature using animation to illustrate different pieces of classical music. Critics argue that the film summarises the best and worst of Disney's art; on the one hand, technically brilliant and visionary; on the other the epitome of misjudgment and bad taste. A key film in addressing the relationship between high art and popular culture.
	Variations	John and James Whitney create experimental animation allied to synthetic electronic sound tracks.
	Superman	The Fleischer Brothers introduce a series of hyper-realist, modern graphic cartoons featuring Superman, taking on mad scientists and machines which operate as thinly veiled metaphors for the Axis enemies, and foreign 'otherness' in general. The $100,000 budgets were over four times the amount spent on comparitive cartoons, but resulted in highly persuasive work which oscillated between comic book graphics, modernist abstraction, and naturalistic verisimilitude.
	The Passengers of the Great Bear	French master animator Paul Grimault's debut film. Grimault's assured narratives echo the poetic realism of other French artists like Renoir. *The King and Mister Bird* (1980) feature is arguably the zenith of his social and artistic vision; *The Revolving Table* (1988), an affecting compilation of his short films.
	Ferda the Ant	Hermìna Tyrlová's puppet film made in Prague. Wife of Karel Dodal, the maker of Czechoslovakia's first puppet animation, *The Lantern's Secret* (1935), Tylová enjoyed a long career in children's animation.

	The Fox and the Crow	Frank Tashlin makes an outstanding cartoon for Columbia's *Screen Gems* series.
		The Disney Strike effectively ends the first 'Golden Era' of the animated cartoon in the United States. Disney himself becomes disaffected and distracted from the core business of making animated films, and works with the government on its 'Good Neighbour' initiative in South America, ultimately making *South of the Border* (1942), *Saludos Amigos* (1942) and *The Three Cabelleros* (1944). Others involved in the strike work for other studios, and UPA (United Productions of America) effectively becomes the first radical splinter group, not merely to oppose the Disney economy and policy, but its aesthetic. UPA modernises the cartoon short.
1942	*Mouse of Tomorrow*	Partly parodying Superman and Mickey Mouse, Paul Terry's 'Terrytoons' introduce Mighty Mouse.
	Weather-Beaten Melody	Hans Fischerkoesen may be regarded as one of the most important artists working in Germany during the war. His films, while embodying the technological advances and artistic expertise which came from government investment, also included a subversive metaphoric undercurrent which implicitly challenged the principles of National Socialism and the Nazi regime. *The Snowman* (1943) and *The Silly Goose* (1945) also embody this approach.
	The Dover Boys	Chuck Jones' under-valued cartoon which anticipates the modernist principles of the UPA studio in the post-war period. Jones uses 'smear' animation to move more abstract figures from extreme pose to extreme pose, using a more limited animation style to counterpoint the clipped literalism of the story he is telling.
	The New Spirit *Der Fuerher's Face*	Disney's war-time propaganda shorts feature Donald Duck, the studio's most popular character. *The New Spirit* encouraged prompt income tax payment, while *Der Fuerher's Face* (1943) satirised 'Nutziland', positing the dangers for the United States if it were to be overcome by the Axis powers. Disney animation was also used in Frank Capra's *Why We Fight* series throughout the war.
		Paramount 'buy out' the Fleischer Brothers and establish 'Famous Studios', but continue to produce the popular Popeye and Superman cartoons. The *Superman* series makes a significant transition from more fantastical, science fictional themes and metaphors, to more literal wartime preoccupations.
1943	*Hen Hop*	Norman McLaren establishes the Animation Unit at the National Film Board of Canada, one of the world's most significant producers of innovative and amusing animation thereafter. As a student, McLaren made *Hell Unltd* (1936); progressed to work with John Grierson at the GPO Film Unit; found financing in New York for *Rumba* (1939) and *Stars and Stripes* (1939), before joining Mary Ellen Bute to make *Spook Sport* (1940). Employed by Grierson again in Canada he made propaganda films including *V for Victory* (1941) and *Hen Hop* (1943), before leading the Animation Unit on *Alouette* (1944). His continually experimental style underpinned indigenous works like *The Young Grey Hen* (1947), which prioritised metamorphosis as its narrative technique in the process of travelling through time.
	Red Hot Riding Hood	Tex Avery consolidates his key themes of sex, speed, status and Disney-bashing in this modern revision of the fairytale.
	Dumb-Hounded	Tex Avery makes the first Droopy cartoon, but it was not until *Northwest Hounded Police* (1946) that Avery fully exploits the tension between Droopy's intrinsic stillness and laconic style, and the exaggerated extremes of the cartoon form. Contemporary animator, Bill Plympton, argues that this becomes a new kind of

		abstraction and extensively exploits the fullest exaggeration of human fears and desires. Avery's work may be viewed as *absurdist* in its attention to black humour and the breakdown of social structures, and the aesthetic structures that embrace them. *King Size Canary* (1947) and *Bad Luck Blackie* (1949) may be seen as the epitome of this style.
	Coal Black and de Sebben Dwarfs	Bob Clampett's take on the Snow White story featuring a range of black caricatures, which on the one hand may be viewed as a film of its time, featuring exemplary performances by black artists and unequalled animation, while on the other may be seen as the perpetuation of racial stereotypes. In many senses the inevitable product of a racist culture, unknowingly reinforcing established cultural tropes while at the same time privileging the undoubted talents of black entertainment figures. Cab Calloway and Louis Armstrong had much earlier been featured in Betty Boop cartoons; the films serving as advertising trailers for forthcoming live performances in the same cities as they were shown.
	SNAFU	Warner Bros. make the 'SNAFU' (Situation Normal All 'Fouled' Up) cartoons for the armed services featuring an inept recruit, Private Snafu who was laughed at, and served as a clear example of what *not* to do. More affecting, if problematic Warner Bros. propaganda could be seen in *Daffy the Commando* (1943), *Herr meets Hare* (1944), *Plane Daffy* (1944) and famously, *Bugs Bunny Nips the Nips* (1944) with its controversial 'grenade ice creams'.
	Momotaro, the Brave Sailor	Mitsuyo Seo, an assistant director to Kenzo Masaoka, maker of the first sound animation in Japan – *The World of Power and Women* (1932) – went on to make propaganda films which challenged and reversed the American perspective. Versed in the work he made for the Sino-Japanese conflict – *The Assault Troops of Sankichi the Monkey* (1935) – he made *Momotaro, the Brave Sailor*, and a sequel, *Momotaro, Divine Sailor* (1944), the first Japanese full-length feature.
	Daffy's Southern Exposure	Leon Schlesinger, the pioneering if 'hands-off' producer of Warner Bros. cartoons sells his studio to them. All Looney Tunes and Merrie Melodies were produced in colour thereafter.
1944	The *Animaland* series	GB Animation, founded by the Rank Organisation, opens in Cookham, led by key ex-Disney figure, David Hand, who had directed *Snow White and the Seven Dwarfs* and *Bambi*. Though in quasi-Disney style, the *Animaland* series, featuring Ginger Nutt, was unsuccessful.
	Hell Bent For Election	The Industrial Film and Poster Service, the forerunners to UPA made up of ex-Disney personnel Steve Bosustow, Dave Hilberman and Zack Schwartz, were commissioned by the Auto-Workers-CIO to make a propaganda film on behalf of Franklin Delano Roosevelt. The short was produced by Steve Bosustow, later a founder of UPA, and directed by Chuck Jones.
	Screwball Squirrel	Tex Avery introduces the mad-cap Screwy Squirrel, who begins this cartoon by taking the archetypal Disney bunny behind a tree and beating it up!
1945	*Casper the Friendly Ghost*	Famous Studios introduce a perennial favourite, recently revived in a full-length feature film.
	Odor-able Kitty	Chuck Jones creates the first Pepe Le Pew cartoon.
	Life with Feathers	Friz Freleng creates the first Sylvester cartoon. Sylvester was a fully developed character debuting in his first story, while his erstwhile partner, Tweety featured in *A Tale of Two Kitties* (1942), *Birdie and the Beast* (1944) and *A Gruesome Twosome* (1945), before the team were paired in *Tweetie Pie* (1947).
1946	*Song of the South*	Disney's controversial part-animated, part-live-action re-telling of

		the 'Uncle Remus' stories, which attracted National Association for the Advancement of Coloured People (NAACP) protest.
	The Brotherhood of Man	UPA established, producing a racially sensitive film which brought the studio to national attention. The shortsighted Mr Magoo became an instant success in *Ragtime Bear* (1949), and was one of the studio's most enduring characters.
		ENIAC, the world's first programmable electronic computer. is introduced by the US military at the University of Pennsylvania.
1947	*Motion Painting #1*	Fischinger uses oil paint on plexiglass to animate colour and form synchronised to Bach's 'Brandenburg Concerto'.
	A Girl at Dojo's Temple	Japanese master, Kon Ichikawa's puppet feature adaptation from a Kabuki Theatre piece.
	Transmutation	Jordan Belson, one of America's West Coast avant-garde completes a silent black and white movement painting on film. *Mambo, Caravan, Mandala, Bop Scotch* (1952–53) and *Flight* (1958), *Raga* (1959) and *Seance* (1959) followed, all exploring some aspect of animation, before Belson moved on to *Allures* (1961) and other real-time photography experiments. Influenced in the 1960s by space flight, Jungian psychology, Eastern philosophies and counter-culture activities, Belson argued that his films, like those of Lye, McLaren and the Whitneys were not 'abstract', but *concrete* in the specificity of their aesthetic, philosophical and material purpose.
	The Czech Year	Jiri Trnka's puppet animation signals the rise of a new Eastern European animated tradition, later continued in the work of Jiri Barta and Jan Svankmajer. Trnka made the controversial *Springer and the SS* (1946) depicting the Nazis as homosexuals (specifically targeting Head of the Blackshirts, Ernst Rohm); the indigenous *Old Czech Legends* (1957); the lavish *Midsummer Night's Dream* (1959); and the anti-authoritarian, pro-art tract *The Hand* (1965).
	The Humpbacked Little Horse	Ivan Ivanov-Vano's playful folktale feature established him as an public favourite and an important cultural commentator in the Soviet Union.
1949	*Little Rural Riding Hood*	Tex Avery modernises and critiques Disney's pre-war preoccupation with town and country themes.
	Fast and Furry-ous	Chuck Jones makes the first of his existential fables featuring the Roadrunner and Wile E. Coyote.
	Begone Dull Care	Norman McLaren's experimental film described by painter Pablo Picasso as 'Finally, something new'.
	Crusader Rabbit	The first cartoon made specifically for television by Jay Ward and Alex Anderson, the former of whom, went on to make the successful *Rocky and Bullwinkle* (1959).
1951	*Gerald McBoing-Boing*	Robert 'Bobe' Cannon and UPA radicalise the cartoon, using modern art principles and new conceptions of story-telling to challenge the dominance of the Disney, Warner Bros. and MGM style. This new graphic style wins an Oscar.
1952	*Neighbours*	Norman McLaren's anti-war film, using *pixillation* – the animation of live-action movement frame by frame.
1953	*The Beast from 20,000 Fathoms*	Ray Harryhausen creates extraordinary 3D creature animation, elevating a throw-away 'B' movie to commercial and artistic success. Harryhausen's animation, like Willis O'Brien's before him, was not properly acknowledged as animated art, and was made 'invisible' by being absorbed into an effects tradition.
	Toot, Whistle, Plunk, and Boom	Disney's short history of music adopts a similarly modern graphic style to UPA. Disney ultimately disapproved of this approach, as it was significantly different from the established Disney aesthetic,

		although it did win the Oscar. Critics have also argued that both UPA and Disney were significantly influenced by Hector Hoppin and Anthony Gross's British-made film, *Joie De Vivre* (1934).
	The Tell-Tale Heart	UPA's adaptation of the Edgar Allan Poe story using animation to depict psychological states through modernist graphic stylings.
	Duck Amuck	Chuck Jones' deconstruction of the cartoon form, or alternatively the humiliation of Daffy Duck by Bugs Bunny ... again!
	One Glass Too Many	Bretislav Pojar's puppet animation warning against the ills of alcohol.
	Melody	The introduction of 3D cartoons, with the 'Adventures in Music' short released by Disney.
1954	*Animal Farm*	Halas and Batchelor releases a persuasive full-length feature adaptation of Orwell's parable about the Russian Revolution.
		Disney closes its cartoon shorts division.
1955	*Yantra*	James Whitney, brother of John, makes a visual tour-de-force optical invention which seeks to evoke the spiritual agenda of the 'sacred machine' alluded to in the title. A similar film, *Lapis* (1963–66) develops this process further.
	Gumbasia	Art Clokey's abstract clay animation, which anticipated his 'Gumby' television series.
		John and Faith Hubley form 'Storyboard' Studios, advance animation practices, and create films addressing global social problems and the particular needs of children. *The Adventures of an* * (1956), funded by the Guggenheim Museum, proved especially popular.
		Paul Terry sells 'Terrytoons' to CBS; Gene Dietch restructures the studio encouraging the work of Ernest Pintoff: *Flebus* (1955) and Jules Feiffer: *Another Day, Another Doormat* (1955).
1956	*One Froggy Evening*	Typical of many Chuck Jones cartoons in combining comic innovation with complex themes which repay analysis and discussion. Here a frog only performs for his owner, but resists all attempts by his owner to commercially exploit his talents. An engaging discourse on communication and capital cultures.
	The Playful Robot	Zagreb Studios established, prioritising modernist art principles in its 'reduced animation' strategy. Dusan Vukotic's film was the first released by the studio.
		MGM closes its short cartoons unit.
1957	*What's Opera, Doc?*	Chuck Jones's classic compression of Wagner's 14-hour 'Ring' cycle into seven minutes. Recently voted as the greatest cartoon of all time by 1,000 animation professionals.
	Once Upon a Time	Jan Lenica and Walerian Borowczyk work on two films, pioneering a collage technique, and using sound as a non-synchronous counterpointing device in advancing satirical points.
	Ruff and Reddy	Hanna Barbera usher in the era of television animation, and the cost-effective 'limited animation' processes that drew from the UPA and Zagreb aesthetic, but found less favour with the artists of the'Golden Era'. Chuck Jones, for example, saw television animation as 'illustrated radio', as the priority for this work was its script rather than its animation *per se*.
		Having made award-winning animations with his brother James in the late 1940s, John Whitney created the first primitive analogue computer graphics. Four years later he creates a television title sequence using this technique. Whitney also worked with the renown Saul Bass on the title sequence for Alfred Hitchcock's film, *Vertigo* (1958). Bass, as well as creating title sequences, made

Year	Title	Description
		Why Man Creates (1968).
1958	*Knighty Knight Bugs*	Bugs Bunny's only Oscar-winning cartoon short.
1959	*1001 Arabian Knights*	UPA makes its first full-length feature.
1960	*Heaven and Earth Magic*	An extraordinary extended film artwork made over ten years between 1950 and 1960 by Harry Smith, one of the post-war West Coast avant-garde group. Influenced by Oscar Fischinger, and sometimes producing work similar to McLaren or Lye, Smith's work is finally its own stream-of-consciousness combination of symbolic and metaphoric images.
	The Flintstones	Hanna Barbera's *The Flintstones* becomes the first animated primetime sit-com, and a vindication of the company's cost effective reduced animation techniques. By this time the studio had also established Huckleberry Hound and Yogi Bear as national stars.
	Goliath II	Disney uses the Xeroxing process in its production for the first time, and uses it throughout its feature *101 Dalmations* (1961). Critics suggested that it either enhanced its Ronald Searle-like graphic style, or created an unpersuasive, 'un-Disney' style.
1961	*Baron Munchausen*	Czechoslovakia's Méliès, Karel Zemen, adapts Gottfried Bürger's novel, in Doré's graphic engraving style, consolidating his innovatory work in animating glass in *Inspiration* (1948) and the Jules Verne-influenced *Invention of Destruction* (1958).
	Ersatz	Zagreb artist Dusan Vukotic's film becomes the first animated short from outside the United States to win the Academy Award.
1962		Ivan Sutherland at MIT creates 'Sketchpad', a software program with enhanced computer graphics.
1963	*Jason and the Argonauts*	Probably the zenith of Harryhausen's career, including a sequence in which the Argonauts do battle with six animated skeletons.
	The Nose	Alexander Alexieffe's adaptation of a Nicolai Gogol short story, based on his re-interpretation of the story through illustrations.
	Astro Boy	The first Japanese animated series to appear on American television, directed by Osamu Tezuka at Mushi Animation Studio. The Japanese animation industry expanded with the production of animation specifically for television broadcast: the Mushi, Tatsanuko (*Ace, the Space Boy* (1965)), TCJ (*Steelman No 28* (1965)) and Toei Studios (*Ken, the Wolf Boy* (1965)) all producing work. By 1983, Japanese studios were producing over 400 television series which found major markets in Europe and Asia. Sub-contracting to Korean studios increased, and major live-action Japanese studios distributed more animated films. Post-1985, the video market encouraged the production of material with more explicit sexual and violent themes. By 1987, up to 100 features/sub-features were produced a year, alongside an expansive affiliated merchandising business.
1964	*Johnny Quest*	Voted as the best Science Fiction Children's cartoon by American critics, Johnny's global adventures were recognised as a serious engagement with the progressive role of science and scientists.
	The Pink Phink	The first DePatie/Freleng 'Pink Panther' cartoon for theatrical distribution.
1965	*Elegy*	Zagreb film-maker Nedeljko Dragic explores the absurdist world of finding humour in paranoia, oppression and loss. *Passing Days* (1969) and *The Day I Quit Smoking* (1982) also exemplify these themes.
		Les Goldman and Bill Littlejohn create the 'Tournée of Animation', an annual touring programme of global animation, seen by the American animation community and arts audiences throughout

		the United States.
1966	*The Fly*	Marks and Jutriša are the Kafkaesque animators of the Zagreb School, concentrating on fears and anxieties of atrophy and loss.
	Superman	Filmation introduces another version of the superhero cartoon. Marvel Comics announced five new television-syndicated cartoons would be made using the Xerox process, featuring *Ironman, The Incredible Hulk, The Mighty Thor, Captain America* and *Sub-Mariner*. Filmation were also notable for their commitment to employeeing only American citizens, when a great deal of animation in the United States was being contracted to Korean studios making work more cost effectively.
	Mr Rossi Buys a Car	Bruno Bozzetto's Italian 'little man' survives in a modern world he is increasingly at odds with. Bozzetto's collaborator, Guido Manuli is similarly influenced by the American 'gag' tradition, which features in *Use Instructions* (1989). Both also share a commitment to ecological and environmental concerns.
		Walt Disney dies on December 15th.
1967	*Pas de Deux*	Norman McLaren's masterpiece – the animation and photographic manipulation of a dance sequence. McLaren viewed all his animations as affiliated to dance.
	Théâtre de M. et Mme Kabal	Walerian Borowcyck's disturbing tale of alienation and atrophy; an extended critique of the machine age and the dehumanisation of the modern world. Politically committed; aesthetically intense.
		Terrytoons/Paramount close their animation studios.
1968	*Permutations*	John Whitney's computer-generated masterpiece made during a period of research for IBM. Whitney felt he had tried to ally new technology to the composition of visual music.
	The Kidnapping of the Sun and Moon	Sando Reisenbüchler's adaptation of a Ferenc Juhasz poem depicting the horror of humankind resisting a monster destroying the earth.
	Thank You Mask Man	John Magnuson and Jeff Hale's animation of a Lenny Bruce routine based on the 'Lone Ranger' scenario, which provokes audiences to think about their homophobia.
	The Yellow Submarine	George Dunning and his British-based team radicalise the animated feature using The Beatles' songs, modern graphic design principles, and the full embrace of counter-culture activities and outlook. Ex-National Film Board of Canada director, Dunning become renown through *Grim Pastures* (1948), *Three Blind Mice* (1945), and *Cadet Rouselle* (1946) with Colin Low, and later with *Flying Man* (1962), *The Maggot* (1973), *Damon the Mower* (1972), and fragments of an uncompleted version of Shakespeare's 'The Tempest'.
1969	*Godzilla Meets Bambi*	Vancouver's Marv Newland crushes Bambi with Godzilla's giant foot, and with it trashes the Disney aesthetic, promotes comic culture, and embraces Japanese exploitation aesthetics. Newland's sense of the bizarre continues with a singer/pianist crooning 'I'm Mad' in *Sing Beast, Sing* (1980), and in the compilation film illustrating a sexually-suggestive soundtrack in *Pink Konkommer* (1990).
	Scooby Doo	One of Hanna Barbera's most popular and enduring cartoon characters.
		Experimental animator Jules Engel heads the department of animation at the influential California Institute of the Arts (CalArts). His films, *Accident* (1973) and *Wet Paint* (1977), remain important abstract experiments, the first a deconstruction of photo-realisminto graphic idioms; the second enhanced by being produced on blotting paper.

		Warner Bros. cease the theatrical distribution of cartoons.
1970	*Australian History*	Bruce Petty's hilarious deadpan illumination of the history of Australia in relation to shifts in global political agendas.
	Alunissons	Swiss animators Ernest and Gisèle Ansorge pioneer working with sand on a whiteboard to achieve an engraving-like effect in their science fiction-style absurdist shorts.
1972	*Fritz the Cat*	Ralph Bakshi radicalises American cartoon animation by the explicit depiction of adult themes and behaviour in the guise of his counter-culture cat. He continued his counter-cultural use of animation in the controversial *Heavy Traffic* (1973) and *Coonskin* (1975).
		Walter Lantz's studio closes, having been one of the longest surviving from the 'Golden Era'.
		George Gerbner's research group finds that animated cartoons are the most violent television genre. Cartoons have perpetually been included in Effects debates on children, though research has been inconclusive. In recent years, there has been greater recognition that children understand the artifice of animation, and that there are different degrees of affect in particular narratives.
1973	*The Wild Planet*	René Laloux and Roland Torpor's existentialist science fantasy feature using surrealist concepts.
1974	*Sisyphus*	Hungarian Marcell Jankovics depicts the Herculian struggle of a man pushing a boulder to the top of a hill, only to see it fall, and to have to make the climb again. An exemplary example of how the graphic line can support the illusion of weight, stress, flow and material effort while carrying the metaphoric weight of Camus' distillation of the absurdist myth.
		John Whitney Jnr continues his father's work, establishing a company to explore the possibilities of 3D CGI for entertainment applications.
1975	*Quasi at the Quackadero*	Sally Cruickshank's revisionist view of the classic cartoon substituting an underground comic sensibility coupled with a feminine perspective on sexual mores and obsessiveness.
	GREAT	Veteran Bob Godfrey's inspired musical documentary of Isambard Kingdom Brunel, featuring innuendo, pathos and politics – the calling-cards of Godfrey's long career in British animation. *Kama Sutre Rides Again* (1971); *Millennium – the Musical* (2000); and *The Many Lives of Norman Spittal* (2000) are testament to his commitment to iconoclasm and irony in the animated film.
		Evan & Sutherland Computer Co. produce the first fully computer-generated images to the United States Maritime Administration for research and development in training situations. The company had been established in 1968 to develop and exploit burgeoning CG technologies.
		George Lucas founds Industrial Light and Magic to create computer-controlled effects for *Star Wars*.
	Closed Mondays	Will Vinton establishes 'Claymation' as a cross-over method between cartoon principles and avant garde modern art expression, radicalising both.
1976	*Dojoji Temple*	Master puppet animator, Kihachiro Kawamoto's Noh-inspired tragedy, which, like *The She-Devil* (1972) and *The House in Flames* (1979) works as explorations of Japanese artistic and mythological traditions.
	The Street	Caroline Leaf's adaptation of Mordecai Richler's auto-biographical writings uses a sand-on-glass metamorphosis technique which

		enhances the representation of recollection and stream-of-consciousness association. Her *The Metamorphosis of Mr Samsa* (1977) summates Kafka persuasively, while *The Two Sisters* (1990), like much of her work, explores female creativity and contradictory emotions of jealousy, passion, and repressed longing.
	Raggedy Ann and Andy	The International Telephone and Telegraph Company fund Richard Williams' film in order to revive the animation industry. This was an unsuccessful initiative.
1977	*Bead Game*	Ishu Patel's aesthetic re-telling of a political event – the Indian Government's experimental explosion of an atomic bomb.
	The Sandcastle	Co Hoedeman's sand creatures build their own castle. An adept use of unusual material to animate in 3D.
	In Plain Sight	Jane Aaron's mix of animation and live action engages with the relationship between the environment, landscape, perception and its embrace in 'feminised' artworks. One of a number of women animators who have used animation to define a distinctive 'feminine aesthetic' that challenges the masculine orthodoxies of live-action cinema. *Interior Designs* (1980) and *Remains to be Seen* (1983) develop this trend.
1978	*Crossing the Atlantic By Rowing Boat*	Jean-François Laguionie's Seurat-inflected cut-out animation tale of a perverse psychological and emotional journey.
	Satiemania	Zdenko Gasparovic's extraordinarily erotic and grotesque invocation of graphic imagery to piano pieces by Erik Satie. The piece has the feel of an underground comic interpretation of stream-of-consciousness perceptions and inarticulable feelings.
	Harpya	Belgian Raoul Servais' brilliant evocation of the close relationship between horror and humour involving a gluttonous, androgynous harpy persecuting the man who saves him. Servais works in multiple styles – *Chromophobia* (1965), an influence on Dunning's *Yellow Submarine*; *Sirène* (1968), a critique of industrial culture; and *Goldframe* (1969), a satire on the film industry, testament to his variety.
	LMNO	Robert Breer's constructivist animation, made with simple images on file cards, engages with simplified circular narratives, stream-of-consciousness, and associative images.
	Asparagus	Arguably one of the finest animated films of all time, Suzan Pitt's challenging piece vividly explores the creative process of women artists in sensual colours and provocative imagery. The underpinning theme of 'feeling and expressing what you cannot see' is played out through the central metaphor of the asparagus.
	Ubu	Geoff Dunbar adapts Jarry's piece, retaining its brutalism and vulgarity.
	Cartoon-A-Torials	Hal Seeger makes a series of animated shorts about social and political issues for educational contexts, sponsored and distributed by *Newsweek*
		Craig Decker and Mike Gribble form Mellow Manor Productions, a streetwise underground promotions company that literally took to the streets to distribute hand bills about pop concerts and animation programmes. In 1991 they created 'The All Sick and Twisted Festival', and supported Mike Judge's first cartoon, *In Bred Jed's Cartoon* (1991), and later, *Frog Baseball* (1992) and *Peace, Love and Understanding* (1993), featuring the fledgling Beavis and Butthead. The Festival has remained popular and is an important event in debuting new work, and expanding the parameters of representation in animated forms.
1979	*Elbowing*	Paul Driessen's symbolic homage to non-conformism, the underpinning imperative of much of the black humour in his

		absurdist films.
	Tale of Tales	Voted as the greatest animated film of all time by fellow animators, Yuri Norstein's elegaic contemplation of childhood, memory and indigenous cultures has a luminescent Rembrandt-like aura, and works as a vindication of art as the most truthful embodiment of human feeling. Norstein is the Andrei Tarkovsky of animated cinema.
	Lineage	George Griffin reflects on the process of animation while exploring his own process as an artist. This was anticipated in his earlier films, *Trikfilm III* (1973), *The Club* (1975) and *Block Print* (1977).
		Don Bluth and a number of colleagues leave the Disney studio in protest at the decline of standards and investment. Bluth establishes his own studio and seeks to continue the Disney tradition in more classical style.
1980		Friz Freleng makes compilations of Warner Bros. cartoons with additional links.
1982	*Tango*	Zbigniew Rbyczynski's multi-charactered fugue, using a cel-photographed cut-out technique plays out the centrality of 'cycles' in animated movement to encompass multiple, potentially related narrative strands.
	Tron *Star Trek: The Wrath of Khan*	The first full-length features to include 3D computer animation. *Tron*'s self-reflexive engagement with a narrative based in a computer itself, and its pioneering aesthetic, proved too innovative for Disney audiences.
	Dimensions of Dialogue	Czech Jan Svankmajer's masterpiece of political allegory part-based on the mannerist style of Prague painter, Archimboldo. Svankmajer's 'militant surrealism' and commitment to using the complex tactile and associative nature of objects, figures in his films from *The Last Trick* (1964) to *Jabberwocky* (1971); *The Death of Stalinism in Bohemia* (1988) to *Conspirators of Pleasure* (1996).
	The Great Cognito	Will Vinton's stand-up 'claymation' with metamorphosing heads works both as a critique and celebration of the United States confusion of fantasy and reality in the conduct of war and foreign policy initiatives.
	The Secret of NIMH	Don Bluth's repost to declining Disney standards.
	Channel Four Logo	Channel Four in Britain uses pioneering CGI logo. Channel Four becomes a significant sponsor, funder and promoter of animation in Britain.
1983	*Bottom's Dream*	Animation historian, teacher and film-maker John Canemaker's short animated adaptation of Shakespeare's 'A Midsummer Night's Dream'.
1984	*Wild Things*	The Disney Studio produces its first computer animation test short. The studio included a computer generated scene in Ron Clements and John Musker's feature *Basil – The Great Mouse Detective* (1986), making a further experimental short, *Oilspot and Lipstick* (1987), a year later. In 1988, ten minutes of *Oliver and Company* is computer-generated.
	The Last Starfighter	Over 25 minutes of computer-generated animation was included in this feature adventure.
1985	*The Adventures of Mark Twain*	Will Vinton's feature length claymation casts Twain as a Jules Verne-like American adventurer.
	Heroic Times	Josef Gemes' extraordinary animated oil painting of the conflicts in the late Middle Ages.
	Tony de Peltrie	Students at the University of Montreal took three years to create this emotive short of a pianist singing an emotional torch song. While capturing a human figure successfully, the short merely

		emphasises the difficulties of creating a persuasive human face in CGI. The short did, however, inspire the then industry standard Softimage 3D animation software.
	The Adventures of André and Wally Bee	John Lasseter's first pioneering PIXAR short, seeking to align new computer graphic idioms with the traditional cartooning skills of the 'Golden Era'. Lasseter followed this with *Luxo Jnr* (1986), a witty tale concerning the playfulness of a child-like angle-poise lamp who accidentally bursts the ball it is playing with. Lasseter endows CGI objects with personality and plausibility, anticipating the Oscar winning *Tin Toy* (1989), the prototype for Lasseter's later *Toy Story* movies.
	Broken Down Film	Versatile Japanese *auteur*, Osamu Tezuka's popular deconstruction of American film.
	The Big Snit	Richard Condie's story of a domestic tension set against global apocalypse neatly encompasses the capacity for animation to condense and enhance the exploration of complex themes in an amusing way. Condie's earlier film, *John Law and the Mississippi Bubble* (1978) uses animation to engage effectively with a historical event.
	Brilliance	Robert Abel's CGI advertisement brings CGI into the commercial mainstream. The distinctive software created by Abel was later purchased by Wavefront.
1986	*The Door*	Nina Shorina's puppet allegory about social hierarchy, paranoia and alienation.
	When the Wind Blows	Jimmy Murakami's TVC production of Raymond Brigg's anti-nuclear story. Murakami's political and satiric credentials had been established with his own films, *The Top* (1965), *Good Friends* (1969) and *Death of a Bullet* (1979).
	The Flying Horse	North Korea's Kim Chun Ok directs a version of Kim Li Sung's short story of a warrior repelling invaders. South Korea's Dong-Seo (East-West) Animation studio increasingly produces animation from across the world because of its huge staff and cost effective production methods.
	Laputa, The Flying Island	Japanese feature *auteur* Hayao Miyazaki creates a spiritual masterwork, engaging with childhood innocence, the mystic elevation of 'flight' and the enduring power of nature in an increasingly technologically complex post-lapsarian world. *Cagliostro's Castle* (1979), *Lupin III* (1980), *Nausicaa of the Valley of the Wind* (1984), *My Neighbour Totoro* (1988), *Porco Rosso* (1992), and *Princess Mononoke* (1999) are all testament to Miyazaki's consistency in his portrayal of strong-willed heroines; the importance of spiritual investment and human feeling; and the preservation of value and purpose in a post-war, post-modern Japan, uncertain of its identity, caught between its contemplative past and its high-tech, urban future.
	Girls' Night Out	Joanna Quinn's hilarious film featuring the middle-aged Welsh housewife Beryl, on a mischievous night out at a male stripshow. Simultaneously, a timely reversal of the 'male gaze'. Quinn's work, including *Body Beautiful* (1988) and *Britannia* (1996) is also part of a vanguard of British female animators – Candy Guard, Erica Russell, Sarah Kennedy, Marjut Rimmenen and Ruth Lingford – defining a ground-breaking 'feminine aesthetic' in film-making practice using animation during the 1980s.
	Street of Crocodiles	The Quay twins adaptation of a Bruno Schulz short story, embodying their engagement with anti-narrative and the process of *re-animation* of the assumed narratives in objects, detritus and uncertain environments. The brothers' films reference peripheral and unconventional strands of European fine arts and literature.

1987	*The Black Dog*	Unsung animator and artist Alison de Vere's dreamlike philosophical enquiry into the relationship between feminine creativity and mythic narratives addressing provocative knowledge uses animation as an act of personal discovery. *Two Faces* (1969), *Cafe Bar* (1975) and *Mr Pascal* (1979) have a similar symbolic, parable-like quality.
	The Man Who Planted Trees	Frédéric Back's story of Elzeard Bouffier, whose efforts in planting a forest on barren land are echoed in Back's pencil pastoral, which captures the integrity, beauty and moral certitude of the endeavour. Back's ecological and aesthetic commitment may also be seen in *Tout Rien* (1979), *Crac!* (1980) and *The Mighty River* (1995).
	Mighty Mouse: The New Adventures	Ralph Bakshi, and among his colleagues, John Kricfalusi, later to find fame with *The Ren and Stimpy Show*, make a new series of Mighty Mouse adventures, modernising the mouse, and making many pop cultural references. The series ended, however, when Bakshi and his team were accused of 'smuggling in' subversive images of cocaine ingestion.
1988	*Picnic on the Grass*	Estonian Priit Pärn's Manet pastiche, which works as an indictment of Soviet oppression and authoritarianism. His earlier film, *Some Exercises for an Independent Life* (1980), considers the relationship between a utilitarian adult and a spontaneous child. His concern for familial relationships continues in *The Triangle* (1981).
	The Cat Came Back	Cordell Barker's 'Roadrunner'-like re-working of the cartoonal indestructability of a character – a cat – and the transition of the victimiser – Mr Johnson – into victim.
	Akira	Katsuhiro Otamo's breakthrough *animé*, depicting a violent post-apocalyptic world, and state-of-the-art sequences of science-fictional invention. Though Otamo's *Roujin Z* (1991) is of a quieter order, it works as a radical enquiry about Japan in transition, seeking to reconcile its past and present.
	Who Framed Roger Rabbit	Robert Zemeckis and Richard Williams' then state-of-the-art combination of cartoon and live-action, celebrating the 'Golden Era' of cartoon production by combining many cartoon characters from different studios in one film. Donald and Daffy Duck, for example, share the same stage for the first time.
		The 'Outrageous Animation' Festival emerges out of the 'Tournée' initiative which had been extant since 1965, and endured in various guises privileging each development in animated and avant-garde cinema. The Festival featured Bob Godfrey's *Instant Sex* and Michel Ocelot's *Four Wishes*. The 'Too Outrageous Animation' programme premiered in 1994.
1989	*The Little Mermaid*	First of the Ron Clements/John Musker trilogy – with *Aladdin* (1992) and *Hercules* (1997) – which re-inspired Disney's fortunes in the feature market place by returning to a 'classical' style but augmenting it with what was traditionally a Warner Bros.-type 'knowingness' and irony.
	The Abyss	The 'pseudopod' created for James Cameron's *The Abyss* by ILM anticipates Cameron's *Terminator 2: Judgement Day* in foregrounding the use of CGI as a character/narrative device in its own right. ILM's work won the Best Special Effects Oscar in 1992.
1990	*The Simpsons*	America's most dysfunctional family radicalise the American sit-com, and return animation to Prime Time for the first time since *The Flintstones*. Significantly, *The Simpsons* challenged *The Cosby Show* in relation to its political stance in representing children and educational issues.
	The Rescuers Down	Disney's aesthetic makes a significant shift in using CGI colouring

	Under	techniques throughout the whole feature.
1991	*Le Crapaud chez ses Beaux Parents*	Zaire's Kibusi Ndjate Wooto's animal fable featuring a toad, and addressing issues about African heritage and the symbolic relationship between humankind and nature.
	Creature Comforts	Nick Park's first Oscar-winning animation, part-zoo documentary, part-hidden camera show, the film established 'Aardman Animation' on the world stage, a company founded by Peter Lord and David Sproxton. Park won further Oscars for *The Wrong Trousers* (1994) and *A Close Shave* (1996). The studio renown for its 'Lip Synch' clay model animation, working in quasi-documentary style, won a five film deal with Dreamworks SKG, completing the first, *Chicken Run* (2000), as a wartime 'Great Escape' parody.
	Mona Lisa Descending a Staircase	An animated history of twentieth-century fine art metamorphosing clay paintings of the masters from Van Gogh to Klee to Warhol.
	The Ren and Stimpy Show	John Kricfalusi's knowing revision of TV era cartoons in the spirit of the more radical work from the 'Golden Era', most particularly, the Fleischer Brothers and Bob Clampett, initially re-vitalises television animation, but is ultimately censured for its provocative and sometimes extreme content
1992	*Beauty and the Beast*	Disney's fairytale becomes the first full-length animated feature to be nominated for an Oscar in the feature section. The film encompasses CGI highly successfully in its ballroom dancing sequence between Belle and the Beast.
		Turner's Cartoon Network begins broadcasting.
1993	*Jurassic Park*	Fully persuasive computer-generated dinosaurs prompt the debate about the ways in which the drive for 'realism' both enhances yet 'hides' the craft of the animator and the art of animation.
	Nightmare Before Christmas	Henry Selick's dark Christmas allegory promotes 3D stop-motion animation as a contemporary feature aesthetic, and features Jack Skellington, a tribute to Harryhausen's skeleton warriors. He also appears in cameo in Selick's Roald Dahl adaptation *James and the Giant Peach* (1995). *Monkey Bone* (2000), another of Selick's part-animated, part live-action vehicles recalls the tone of his earlier work, however, in *Slow Bob in the Lower Dimensions* (1990).
	Reboot	The first fully computer generated animation television series. Ian Pearson, Gavin Blair and Phil Mitchell's pioneering work has been neglected in the light of John Lasseter's phenomenal success in CGI narratives. Living within a computer environment, in the city of Main-frame, Bob, Enzo and their friend Dot Matrix battle two viruses, Megabyte and Hexadecimal.
1994	*The Lion King*	Disney's phenomenally successful 'Hamlet'-influenced African myth did, however, provoke controversy in relation to its representation of 'black' characters. Further, critics and fans argued that it bore a strong, unacknowledged resemblance to Osamu Tezuka's *Kimba the White Lion* (aka *Jungle Emperor* or *Jungle Taitei*) (1965).
	The Grey-Bearded Lion	Russian poet-laureate Andrei Khrzhanovsky's alliance of Felliniesque folk idioms embodied in the circus, and a Yuri Norstein sense of beauty and loss. Khrzhanovsky's versatility is reflected in his earlier films, which include *There Lives a Man Called Kozyavin* (1966), which critiques bureaucracy; his Samuel Marshak translation of the English children's poem, *The House that Jack Built* (1976); his Pushkin trilogy, including the extraordinary *I Am Still With You* (1980); and his A. A. Milne adaptation of *The King's Breakfast* (1985).
1995	*Ghost in the Shell*	Mamoro Oshii's persuasive exploration of post-modern cyber-

culture, addressing post-human identity, and the search for an authentic sense of 'soul' – the 'ghost' in the 21st-century machine.

Toy Story

The first fully computer-generated animation feature film, which won a Special Achievement Oscar in 1996. Featuring Woody, the pull-string cowboy, and Buzz Lightyear, a gadget-laden space astronaut, the film moves beyond its technical achievement and 'buddy' movie veneer, into an engaging address of human feelings and foibles: Woody's jealousy and feelings of redemption; Buzz's identity crisis; their owner Andy's emotional investment in his toys; and his neighbour Sid's perverse creativity.

The Thief and the Cobbler

Richard Williams' thirty-year investment in creating his own auteur vehicle ends in profoundly disappointing circumstances as additional footage and re-editing by new owners and distributors undermines and invalidates the ambition and considerable achievement of the film.

1997 *I Married a Strange Person*

Oregon iconoclast Bill Plympton moves on from his persona as a deadpan Tex Avery in shorts like *Your Face* (1987) and *25 Ways to Give Up Smoking* (1989) to fully consolidate his excessive and surreal depictions of sex and violence, vividly explored in *Sex and Violence* (1998), and here working as a none-too-veiled attack on mediated consumer culture. Plympton writes, produces, directs and animates his own work. *Mutant Aliens* (2001) consolidates his anarchic reputation as an astronaut brings home some alien companions.

A Bug's Life
Antz

John Lasseter's follow up to *Toy Story* re-works *The Seven Samurai* via Fellini, while Dreamworks SKG's *Antz* explores social metaphor in its engagement with the role of the individual in a hierarchical, highly conformist social infrastructure. Dreamworks SKG consolidated their success in animation with the controversial *Prince of Egypt* (1998) which, while creating a state-of-the-art 'parting-of-the Red-Sea' sequence, offended some religious and political sensibilities.

Perfect Moon

Satoshi Kon's adaptation of Yoshikazu Takeuchi's novel re-configures *animé* as an exploration of the paranoia and self-delusion of celebrity and its unstable cultural context.

1999 *Stuart Little*

Part live action, part CGI story, featuring a state-of-the-art computer-generated mouse, who seamlessly integrates with the codes and conventions of his live-action environment.

Walking with Dinosaurs

BBC quasi-documentary series featuring persuasive dinosaurs in their natural habitats.

Gilbert and Sullivan

Barry Purves' exemplary musical biography of Gilbert and Sullivan, using puppet animation. An important interrogation of 'Britishness' and a theatrical tour-de-force.

The Old Man and the Sea

Alexander Petrov's exquisite and evocative tale resituates animation as an emotive and contemplative medium rather than one subject merely to spectacle and technological imposition.

Toy Story 2

John Lasseter's sequel to *Toy Story* advances further the central theme of the first film as the toys resist their own obsolescence, finding their 'human' value as toys rather than material and commercial artefacts. Both films represent an engaging and sometimes critical take on American popular culture in the post-war period.

Pleasures of War

Ruth Lingford's re-configuration of computer technology in the challenging pursuit of illustrating the sometimes inchoate and unspeakable feelings of pleasure which underpin the execution of brutal and inhumane acts.

The Iron Giant

Former *Simpsons* director Brad Bird's adaptation of Ted Hughes's poetic novella explores 1950s Cold War America, using a CGI,

		sub-animé robot to good effect, while also prioritising acting performances in animated characters.
2000	*Father and Daughter*	Michael Dudok de Wit's fable about love, devotion and memory played out in simple graphic style uses animation to invoke the importance of time. His previous work includes the witty *The Monk and the Fish* (1996).
	Dinosaur	Disney's first all-digital feature, which heralded the creation of a new digital facility, and a film respectful of the 'dinosaur' tradition in animation. Over 30 separate species were represented, mapped into real location shots, sometimes using the flexible motion control 'Dino-cam'. New software to generate lemurs' fur was also created. Over 1,300 'naturalistic' character shots mark the film out as a significant development towards computer generated 'realism'.
	The Miracle Maker	Cartwn Cymru (Wales) collaborates with Christmas Films (Moscow) in a child's-eye re-telling of the Jesus story. A high watermark in the continuing collaborations between Welsh and Russian production companies who have achieved an *Animated Shakespeare* series (SC4/Soyuzmultfilms) (1992); *Operavox: The Animated Operas* (SC4/Christmas Films) (1994); *Animated World Faiths* (SC4/Christmas Films) (1998); *Testament* (Cartwn Cymru/ Christmas Films) (1998), based on other Bible stories; and literary adaptations including *Beowulf, Moby Dick, Don Quixote* and *The Canterbury Tales.*
	Zombie College	Internet animation grows exponentially. Icebox on-line animation studio presents the subversive *Zombie College,* created by *Futurama* producer, Eric Kaplan. Unbound Studios consolidate on-line work with Nickelodeon; John Kricfalusi creates animation on his on 'Spumco' website.
	Cyberworld	Hugh Murray's 3D CGI tour around Galleria Animatica, viewed on an IMAX screen, featuring the 3D sequence from *The Simpsons*' 'Treehouse of Horror' (1995) and the bar scene from *Antz.* Other sequences include *Monkey Brain Sushi* (1995), *Krakken: Adventure of Future Ocean* (1997), and the Pet Shop Boys video *Liberation* (1994). A 3D version of Dreamworks SKG's William Steig, ogre myth *Shrek* (2001) followed its traditional 2D distribution.
	Mickey Mouseworks	Mickey returns in his first cartoons since the 1950s.
	Titan AE	Don Bluth's failed post-apocalytic combined-style animated feature allegedly responsible for the closure of Fox's Animation Unit.
	Sinbad: Beyond the Valley of the Mists	India's Pentamedia studio produces the first full-length feature using 'motion capture' – the computer capture of human movement, or what might be termed 'digital rotoscoping' – throughout, but it proves an unpersuasive aesthetic.
2001	*Final Fantasy: The Spirits Within*	Hironobu Sakaguchi's feature using photorealist performance animation, echoing the aesthetic of its video-game source, and enhancing the television series using computer game aesthetics coupled with 'motion capture', *Roughnecks: Starship Troopers Chronicles, Max Steel* and *Dark Justice.*
	Mansion Cat	In the year when 'Hanna' of Hanna Barbera dies, the studio produces its first 'Tom and Jerry' short in nearly forty years. First shown as part of the Cartoon Network's annual 'Tom and Jerry' New Year marathon, the short echoes classics like *Mouse in Manhattan* (1945), *Quiet Please* (1945), and *Solid Seranade* (1946). 'The Itchy and Scratchy Show' in *The Simpsons* is explicitly based on the popular duo's enduring adventures, although the classic 1940–57 Hanna Barbera period should not be confused with the more surreal Gene Dietch productions that followed, nor Chuck Jones's more lyrical, less violent narratives.

Gorillaz

Damon Albarn's 2D cartoon pop-vehicle recalls a whole tradition of animation from the early 1930s onwards in which the illustration of songs is the underpinning aspect of the cartoons. Warner Bros. used songs to advertise their sheet music. The Fleischer Brothers used Cab Calloway and Louis Armstrong songs and performances in cartoons which prefigured their live shows and served as quasi-pop videos. The pop video itself has many fine examples of animation including Peter Lord's 'My Baby Just Cares For Me'. Pop groups have featured, too, including TVC's *The Beatles,* in the mid-1960s, followed quickly by *The Jackson Five* and *The Osmonds* in the early 1970s. The successof 'Gorillaz' prompted the re-release of 'Sugar, Sugar' by the 1970s cartoon group, The Archies.

2002

Chuck Jones dies on February 22nd.

GLOSSARY

anthropomorphism
The tendency in animation to endow creatures with human attributes, abilities and qualities. This can redefine or merely draw attention to characteristics which are taken for granted in live-action representations of human beings.

reduced animation (limited animation)
Animation may be literally the movement of one line which, in operating through time and space, may take on characteristics which an audience may perceive as expressive and symbolic. This form of minimalism constitutes reduced animation, which takes as its premise 'less is more'. Literally an eye movement or the shift of a body posture becomes enough to connote a particular feeling or meaning. This enables the films to work in a mode which has an intensity of suggestion.

metamorphosis
The ability of a figure, object, shape or form to relinquish its seemingly fixed properties and mutate into an alternative model. This transformation is literally enacted within the animated film and acts as a model by which the process of change becomes part of the narrative of the film. A form starts as one thing and ends up as something different.

pixillation
The frame-by-frame recording of deliberately staged live-action movement to create the illusion of movement impossible to achieve by naturalistic means, for ezample figures spinning in mid-air or skating in mid-air. This can also be achieved by particular ways of editing material.

proto-animation
This may be understood as the illusion of animated movement that has been created by other means than its execution or recording on film or disk. Pre-cinematic 'toys' and machines which created the illusion of movement provide the best evidence of this. The Phenakistoscope (1831) was made up of two rotating discs which appeared to make an image move. The Kinematoscope (1861) was more sophisticated and employed a series of sequencial photographs mounted on a wheel and rotated. The Praxinoscope (1877), pioneered by Emile Reynaud, was a strip of images mounted in a revolving drum and reflected in mirrors; a model later revised and renamed Theatre Optique, that may claim to be the first proper mechanism to project seemingly animated images on to a screen. Early live-action cinema demonstrated certain techniques which preceded their conscious use as a method in creating animation. This is mainly revealed in stop-motion photography, mixed media forms and the use of dissolves to create the illusion of metamorphosis in early 'trick' films.

squash 'n' stretch
Many cartoon characters are constructed in a way that resembles a set of malleable and attached circles that may be elongated or compressed to achieve an effect of dynamic movement. When animators 'squash 'n' stretch' these circles they effectively create the physical space of the character and a particular design structure within the overall pattern of the film. Interestingly, early Disney shorts had characters based on 'ropes' rather than circles and this significantly changes the look of the films.

NOTES

CHAPTER ONE

1 In the post-war period, 'Fordism' – the highly efficient production process pioneered by Henry Ford in the mass construction of cars – became a metaphor for the process orientation and regulation of roles within a hierarchy of labour practices in modern, rationalised, corporate businesses. Arguably, this created well-administered and reliable mechanisms of production which facilitated high quality, economically viable, product outputs, and clarified matters of ownership, control, and responsibility.

2 Montage, pioneered in the films of the Soviet directors Eisenstein and Pudovkin, is a mode of editing in which the juxtaposition and counterpointing of one image against another seeks to reveal a particular relationship, provoking particular sensations, or offering insights about the socio-political and ideological issues underpinning the imagery, which are less conscious but fundamental to the practices in public life.

CHAPTER TWO

1 Hanks made these comments in conversation with Mark Cousins in Tom Hanks: Scene By Scene (BBC Television, tx: 20 January 2001).

CHAPTER FOUR

1 For a brief overview of the animated Horror film, see P. Wells (2000) *The Horror Genre: From Beelzebub to Blair Witch*. London: Wallflower Press, 101–4.

2 All the material in this section is informed by an interview with Richard Taylor by the author, 10 May 1999.

3 For an extended discussion of 'environmental' and 'ecological' films produced in Britain, see P. Wells (forthcoming) *British Animation: An Industry of Innovation*. London: British Film Institute.

CHAPTER FIVE

1 Walt Disney in conversation with Fletcher Markle, BBC Recording Transcript, 196: unpaginated; BBC Archives, Broadcasting House, London.

2 Art Babbitt interviewed, BBC Recording Transcript, 1973: 5, BBC Archives, Broadcasting House, London.

3 Ward Kimball in interview with the author, June 1984.

4 Walt Disney interviewed, BBC Recording Transcript, 1973: 2, BBC Archives, Broadcasting House, London.

5 James Cameron speaking in Working with Dinosaurs: Ray Harryhausen (October Films, tx: Channel Four, December 1999).

6 Ray Harryhausen in interview with the author, June 1994.

7 From John Canemaker's introduction to Caroline Leaf at the American Film Institute Walter Lantz Seminar on Animation, 6 November 1988.

8 Caroline Leaf in interview with the author, June 1997.

FILMOGRAPHY

Abductees (Paul Vester, 1994, UK)
The Abyss (James Cameron, 1989, US)
Accident (Jules Engel, 1973, US)
Ace, the Space Boy (Mushi, Tatsanuko, 1965, Jap.)
Achilles (Barry Purves, 1995, UK)
Action After Warnings (Richard Taylor, 1975, UK)
The Adventures of an * (John and Faith Hubley, 1956, US)
The Adventures of André and Wally Bee (John Lasseter, 1985, US)
The Adventures of Mark Twain (Will Vinton, 1985, US)
The Adventures of Prince Achmed (Lotte Reiniger, 1926, Ger.)
Akira (Katsuhiro Otamo, 1988, Jap.)
Aladdin (Ron Clements and John Musker, 1992, US)
Alice in Wonderland (Clyde Geronimi, Hamilton Luske and Wilfred Jackson, 1951, US)
Alice the Dog Catcher (Walt Disney, 1924, US)
Alice's Hunting in Africa (Walt Disney, 1923, US)
Alice's Wild West Show (Walt Disney, 1924, US)
Alice's Wonderland (Walt Disney, 1923, US)
Alien III (David Fincher, 1993, US)
Allegro (Norman McLaren, 1939, UK)
Allures (Jordan Belson, 1961, US)
Alouette (Norman McLaren, 1944, Can.)
Alunissons (Ernest and Gisèle Ansorge, 1970, Switz.)
Animal Farm (John Halas and Joy Batchelor, 1954, UK)
Another Day, Another Doormat (Jules Feiffer, 1955, US)
Antz (Eric Darnell and Lawrence Guterman, 1997, US)
Any Rags (Max Fleischer, 1932, US)
Argument in a Supermarket (Stuart Hinton, 1993, UK)
The Artist's Dream (Earl Hurd, 1913, US)
Asparagus (Suzan Pitt, 1978, US)
The Assault Troops of Sankichi the Monkey (Mitsuyo Seo, 1935, Jap.)
Astro Boy (Osamu Tezuka, 1963, Jap.)
Australian History (Bruce Petty, 1970, Aus.)
Bad Luck Blackie (Fred 'Tex' Avery, 1949, US)
Balance (Christoph and Wolfgang Lauenstein, 1989, Ger.)
Ballet Mécanique (Fernand Léger, 1924, Fra.)
Bambi (Walt Disney and David Hand, 1942, US)
The Band Concert (Walt Disney, 1935, US)
Baron Munchausen (Karel Zemen, 1961, Cz.)
Basil – The Great Mouse Detective (Ron Clements and John Musker, 1986, US)
Bead Game (Ishu Patel, 1977, Can.)

The Beast from 20,000 Fathoms (Eugene Lurie, 1953, US)
Beauty and the Beast (Kirk Wise and Gary Trousdale, 1992, US)
Begone Dull Care (Norman McLaren, 1949, Can.)
Betty Boop's Snow White (Max Fleischer, 1933, US)
Betty Co-Ed (Max Fleischer, 1931, US)
The Big Snit (Richard Condie, 1985, Can.)
The Big Snooze (Bob Clampett, 1946, US)
Biogenesis (William Latham, 1993, UK)
Birdie and the Beast (Bob Clampett, 1944, US)
The Birth of a Robot (Len Lye, 1936, UK)
The Black Dog (Alison de Vere, 1987, UK)
Block Print (George Griffin, 1977, US)
Body Beautiful (Joanna Quinn, 1988, UK)
Bop Scotch (Jordan Belson, 1952–53, US)
Bottom's Dream (John Canemaker, 1983, US)
Brilliance (Richard Abel, 1985, US)
Britannia (Joanna Quinn, 1996, UK)
Broken Down Film (Osamu Tezuka, 1985, Jap.)
The Brotherhood of Man (Robert 'Bobe' Cannon, 1946, US)
A Bug's Life (John Lasseter, 1997, US)
Bugs Bunny Nips the Nips (Isadore 'Friz' Freleng, 1944, US)
Bugs Bunny Rides Again (Isadore 'Friz' Freleng, 1948, US)
Cadet Rouselle (George Dunning, 1946, Can.)
Cafe Bar (Alison de Vere, 1975, UK)
Cagliostro's Castle (Hayao Miyazaki, 1979, Jap.)
The Cameraman's Revenge (Ladislaw Starewich, 1911, Rus.)
Caravan (Jordan Belson, 1952–53, US)
Casper the Friendly Ghost (I. Sparber, 1945, US)
Casualties (Richard Taylor, 1975, UK)
The Cat Came Back (Cordell Barker, 1988, Can.)
The Cavalier's Dream (Thomas Edison, 1898, US)
Charge of the Light Brigade (Tony Richardson, 1963, UK)
Chicken Run (Nick Park and Peter Lord, 2000, UK/US)
A Chord of Colour (Arnaldo Ginna, 1910, It.)
Chromophobia (Raoul Servais, 1965, Bel.)
Clash of the Titans (Desmond Davis, 1981, US/UK)
Clock Cleaners (Walt Disney and Ben Sharpsteen, 1937, US)
A Close Shave (Nick Park, 1996, UK)
Closed Mondays (Will Vinton, 1975, US)
The Club (George Griffin, 1975, US)
Coal Black and de Sebben Dwarfs (Bob Clampett, 1943, US)
A Colour Box (Len Lye, 1935, UK)
Composition in Blue (Oskar Fischinger, 1935, Ger)
Conspirators of Pleasure (Jan Svankmajer, 1996, Cz.)
Coonskin (Ralph Bakshi, 1975, US)
The Country Cousin (Walt Disney, 1936, US)
Cowboys (Phil Mulloy, 1990, UK)
Crac! (Frédéric Back, 1980, Can.)
Creation (Will Vinton, 1981, US)
Creature Comforts (Nick Park, 1991, UK)
Crossing the Atlantic by Rowing Boat (Jean-François Laguionie, 1978, Fr.)
Crusader Rabbit (Jay Ward and Alex Anderson, 1949, US)
The Czech Year (Jiri Trnka, 1947, Cz.)
Daffy the Commando (Isadore 'Friz' Freleng, 1943, US)
Daffy's Southern Exposure (Norman McCabe, 1943, US)
Damon the Mower (George Dunning, 1972, UK)
Dangerous Dan McFoo (Fred 'Tex' Avery, 1939, US)
The Day I Quit Smoking (Nedeljko Dragic, 1982, Yug.)
Deadsy (David Anderson, 1990, UK)
Death and the Mother (Ruth Lingford, 1996, UK)
Death of a Bullet (Jimmy Murakami, 1979, UK)
Death of Stalinism in Bohemia (Jan Svankmajer, 1990, UK/Cz.)

Der Fuerher's Face (Walt Disney, 1943, US)
The Diagonal Symphony (Viking Eggeling, 1922, Ger.)
Dimensions of Dialogue (Jan Svankmajer, 1982, Cz.)
Dinnertime (Paul Terry, 1928, US)
Dinosaur (Eric Leighton and Ralph Zondag, 2000, US)
The Dinosaur and the Missing Link (Willis O'Brien, 1914, US)
The Discontented Canary (Hugh Harman and Rudolph Ising, 1934, US)
Dizzy Dishes (Max Fleischer, 1930, US)
Do-It-Yourself Cartoon Kit (Bob Godfrey, 1961, UK)
Dojoji Temple (Kihachiro Kawamoto, 1976, Jap.)
The Door (Nina Shorina, 1986, Rus.)
The Dover Boys (Chuck Jones, 1942, US)
Dr Jeckyl and Mr Mouse (William Hanna and Joseph Barbera, 1946, US)
Duck Amuck (Chuck Jones, 1953, US)
Dumb-Hounded (Tex Avery, 1943, US)
Earth vs The Flying Saucers (Fred Sears, 1952, US)
Einstein's Theory of Relativity (Max Fleischer, 1923, US)
El Apóstel (Quirino Cristiani, 1917, Arg.)
Elbowing (Paul Driessen, 1979, Can.)
The Electric Hotel (Segundo de Chomòn, 1905, Sp.)
Elegy (Nedeljko Dragic, 1965, Yug.)
El Nombre (Ealing Animation, 1994–present, UK)
The Emperor's New Groove (Mark Dindal, 2001, US)
The Enchanted Drawing (J. Stuart Blackton, 1900, US)
Ersatz (Dusan Vukotic, 1961, Yug.)
Escape (Mary Ellen Bute, 1938, US)
Ever Been Had? (Dudley Buxton, 1917, UK)
Eveready Harton in Buried Treasure (Unknown, 1928, US)
Experiments in Hand Drawn Sound (Oskar Fischinger, 1932, Ger.)
Fantasia (Walt Disney, 1940, US)
Fantasmagorie (Emile Cohl, 1908, Fr.)
Fast and Furry-ous (Chuck Jones, 1949, US)
Father and Daughter (Michael Dudok de Wit, 2000, Fr.)
Feline Follies (Pat Sullivan/Otto Messmer, 1919, US)
Ferda the Ant (Hermina Tyrlovà, 1941, Cz.)
Final Fantasy: The Spirits Within (Hironobu Sakaguchi, 2001, Jap.)
Flatworld (Daniel Greaves, 1998, UK)
Flebus (Ernest Pintoff, 1955, US)
Flight (Jordan Belson, 1958, US)
The Flintstones (William Hanna and Joseph Barbera, 1960, US)
Flowers and Trees (Walt Disney, 1932, US)
The Fly (Aleksandar Marks and Vladimir Jutrisa, 1966, Yug.)
The Flying Horse (Kim Chun Ok, 1986, N. Kor.)
Flying Man (George Dunning, 1962, UK)
The Four Musicians of Bremen (Walt Disney, 1922, US)
Four Wishes (Michel Ocelot, 1988, Fr.)
The Fox and the Crow (Frank Tashlin, 1941, US)
Friday the 13th (Sean Cunningham, 1980, US)
Fritz the Cat (Ralph Bakshi, 1972, US)
Frog Baseball (Mike Judge, 1992, US)
Frolicking Fish (Walt Disney, 1930, US)
Fun in a Bakery Shop (Edwin Porter, 1902, US)
The Gallopin' Gaucho (Walt Disney/Ub Iwerks, 1928, US)
George and Rosemary (Ricard Condie, 1984, Can.)
Gerald McBoing-Boing (Robert 'Bobe' Cannon, 1951, US)
Gertie the Dinosaur (Winsor McCay, 1914, US)
Ghost in the Shell (Mamuro Oshii, 1995, US)
Gilbert and Sullivan (Barry Purves, 1999, UK)
A Girl at Dojo's Temple (Kon Ichikawa, 1947, Jap.)
Girls' Night Out (Joanna Quinn, 1986, UK)
Godzilla Meets Bambi (Marv Newland, 1969, Can.)
The Golden Touch (Walt Disney, 1935, US)

Goldframe (Raoul Servais, 1969, Bel.)
Goliath II (Walt Disney and Wolfgang Reitherman, 1960, US)
Good Friends (Jimmy Murakami, 1969, UK)
GREAT (Bob Godfrey, 1975, UK)
The Great Cognito (Will Vinton, 1982, US)
The Grey Bearded Lion (Andrei Khrzhanovsky, 1994, USSR)
Grim Pastures (George Dunning, 1946, Can.)
Growing (Alison Hempstock, 1994, UK)
A Gruesome Twosome (Bob Clampett, 1945, US)
Gulliver's Travels (Max Fleischer, 1939, US)
Gumbasia (Art Clokey, 1955, US)
Halloween (John Carpenter, 1978, US)
The Hand (Jiri Trnka, 1965, Cz.)
The Happy Moose (Walter Santucci, 1995, US)
Harpya (Raoul Servais, 1978, Bel.)
Heaven and Earth Magic (Harry Smith, 1960, US)
Heavy Traffic (Ralph Bakshi, 1973, US)
Heidi's Horse (Sheila Graber, 1987, UK)
Hell Bent for Election (Chuck Jones, 1944, US)
Hell Unltd (Norman McLaren, 1936, US)
Hen Hop (Norman McLaren, 1943, Can.)
Hercules (Ron Clements and John Musker, 1997, US)
Heroic Times (Josef Gemes, 1985, Hun.)
Herr Meets Hare (Isadore 'Friz' Freleng, 1944, US)
Honeymoon Hotel (Earl Duvall, 1934, US)
House in Flames (Kihachiro Kawamoto, 1979, Jap.)
House of Tomorrow (Fred 'Tex' Avery, 1949, US)
The House That Jack Built (Andrei Khrzhanovsky, 1976, USSR)
How the Beaver Stole Fire (Caroline Leaf, 1971, US)
Humourous Phases of Funny Faces (J. Stuart Blackton, 1906, US)
The Humpbacked Little Horse (Ivan Ivanov-Vano, 1947, USSR)
Humpty Dumpty Circus (J. Stuart Blackton, 1987, US)
The Hungry, Hungry Nipples (Walter Santucci, 1997, US)
I Am Still With You (Andrei Khrzhanovsky, 1980, USSR)
I Haven't Got a Hat (Isadore 'Friz' Freleng, 1935, US)
I Married a Strange Person (Bill Plympton, 1997, US)
I'm No Fool in Water (Walt Disney, 1957, US)
Imokawa Muzuko, the Concierge (Oten Shimokawa, 1917, Jap.)
In Plain Sight (Jane Aaron, 1977, US)
Inbred Jed's Cartoon (Mike Judge, 1991, US)
Inspiration (Karel Zemen, 1948, Cz.)
Instant Sex (Bob Godfrey, 1988, UK)
Interior Designs (Jane Aaron, 1980, US)
Interview (Caroline Leaf and Veronica Soul, 1979, US)
Invention of Destruction (Karel Zemen, 1958, Cz.)
The Iron Giant (Brad Bird, 1999, US)
It Came From Beneath the Sea (Robert Gordon, 1953, US)
Jabberwocky (Jan Svankmajer, 1971, Cz.)
Jack and the Beanstalk (Walt Disney, 1922, US)
James and the Giant Peach (Henry Selick, 1995, US)
Jason and the Argonauts (Nathan Juran, 1963, US)
The Jetsons (William Hanna and Joseph Barbera, 1962, US)
John Bull's Animated Sketchbook (Dudley Buxton and Anson Dyer, 1920, UK)
John Law and the Mississippi Bubble (Richard Condie, 1978, Can.)
Johnny Quest (William Hanna and Joseph Barbera, 1964, US)
Joie De Vivre (Hector Hoppin and Anthony Gross, 1934, UK)
The Jungle Book (Wolfgand Reitherman, 1967, US)
Jurassic Park (Stephen Spielberg, 1993, US)
Kama Sutre Rides Again (Bob Godfrey, 1971, UK)
Ken, the Wolf Boy (Toei, 1965, Jap.)
The Kidnapping of the Sun and Moon (Sando Reisenbüchler, 1968, Hun.)
Kimba the White Lion (Osamu Tezuka, 1965, Jap.)

The King and Mister Bird (Paul Grimault, 1980, Fr.)
King Kong (Merian C. Cooper and Ernest B. Schoedsack, 1933, US)
King of Jazz (John Murray Anderson, 1930, US)
King Size Canary (Fred 'Tex' Avery, 1947, US)
The King's Breakfast (Andrei Khrzhanovsky, 1985, USSR)
Knighty Knight Bugs (Isadore 'Friz' Freleng, 1958, US)
Knock Knock (Walter Lantz, 1940, US)
La Luna (Anna Fodorova and Vera Neubauer, 1999, UK)
Lady Play Your Mandolin (Frank Marsales, 1931, US)
The Lantern's Secret (Karel Dodal, 1935, Cz.)
Lapis (James Whitney, 1963–66, US)
Laputa, The Flying Island (Hayao Miyazaki, 1986, Jap.)
The Last Starfighter (Nick Castle, 1984, US)
The Last Trick (Jan Svankmajer, 1964, Cz.)
The Lazy Sword (Junichi Kouchi, 1917, Jap.)
Le Crapuad chez ses Beaux Parents (Kibusi Ndjate Wooto, 1991, Zr.)
Legacy (Will Vinton, 1979, US)
Lichtspiel Opus 1 (Walter Ruttman, 1921, Ger.)
L'Idee (Berthold Bartosch, 1934, Ger.)
Life with Feathers (Isadore 'Friz' Freleng, 1945, US)
Lineage (George Griffin, 1979, US)
The Lion King (Roger Allers and Rob Minhoff, 1994, US)
The Little Mermaid (Ron Clements and John Musker, 1989, US)
Little Nemo in Slumberland (Winsor McCay, 1911, US)
Little Red Riding Hood (Walt Disney, 1922, US)
Little Rural Riding Hood (Fred 'Tex' Avery, 1949, US)
LMNO (Robert Breer, 1978, US)
The Lost World (Willis O'Brien, 1925, US)
Love on the Wing (Norman McLaren, 1937, UK)
Love Requited (Jan Lenica and Walerian Borowczyk, 1957, Pol.)
Lupin III (Hayao Miyazaki, 1980, Jap.)
Luxo Jnr (John Lasseter, 1986, US)
The Mad Doctor (Walt Disney, 1933, US)
The Maggot (George Dunning, 1973, UK)
Mambo (Jordan Belson, 1952–53, US)
The Man Who Planted Trees (Frédéric Back, 1987, Can.)
Mandala (Jordan Belson, 1952–53, US)
Manipulation (Daniel Greaves, 1991, UK)
Mansion Cat (William Hanna and Joseph Barbera, 2001, US)
The Many Lives of Norman Spittal (Bob Godfrey, 2000, UK)
Mary Poppins (Robert Stevenson, 1967, US)
Matches: An Appeal (Arthur Melbourne Cooper, 1899, UK)
Melody (Walt Disney, Ward Kimball and Charles Nicholls, 1953, US)
The Metamorphosis of Mr Samsa (Caroline Leaf, 1977, Can.)
Midsummer Night's Dream (Jiri Trnka, 1959, Cz.)
Mighty Joe Young (Ernest Schoedsack, 1945, US)
The Mighty River (Frédéric Back, 1995, Can.)
Millennium – The Musical (Bob Godfrey, 2000, UK)
The Miracle Maker (Derek Hayes, 2000, UK)
Momotaro, Divine Sailor (Mitsuyo Seo, 1944, Jap.)
Momotaro, the Brave Sailor (Mitsuyo Seo, 1943, Jap.)
Mona Lisa Descending a Staircase (Joan Gratz, 1991, US)
The Monk and the Fish (Michael Dudok de Wit, 2000, UK)
Monkey Bone (Henry Selick, 2000, US)
Monster City (Yoshiaki Kawajiri, 1987, Jap.)
More Sex and Violence (Bill Plympton, 1998, US)
Motion Picture #1 (Oskar Fischinger, 1947, Ger.)
Mouse in Manhattan (William Hanna and Joseph Barbera, 1945, US)
Mouse of Tomorrow (Paul Terry, 1942, UK)
Mr Pascal (Alison De Vere, 1979, UK)
Mr Peeler's Butterflies (Simon and Sara Bor, 2001, UK)
Mr Rossi Buys a Car (Bruno Bozzetto, 1966, It.)

Mutant Aliens (Bill Plympton, 2001, US)
My Neighbour Totoro (Hayao Miyazaki, 1988, Jap.)
The Naughty Mailbox (Seitaro Kitayama, 1917, Jap.)
Nausicaa of the Valley of the Wind (Hayao Miyazaki, 1984, Jap.)
Neighbours (Norman McLaren, 1952, Can.)
A New Gulliver (Alexander Ptushko, 1935, USSR)
The New Spirit (Walt Disney, 1942, US)
The Newlyweds (Emile Cohl, 1913, US)
Nezha Triumphs Over the Dragon King (Xu Jingda, 1979, Ch.)
Night Angel (Bratislav Pojar and Jacques Drouin, 1988, Can.)
Night Butterflies (Raoul Servais, 1996, Bel.)
Night on Bald Mountain (Alexander Alexeieff and Clare Parker, 1934, Fr.)
Night Visitors (Richard Ollive, 1989, UK)
Nightmare Before Christmas (Henry Selick, 1993, US)
Northwest Hounded Police (Fred 'Tex' Avery, 1946, US)
The Nose (Alexander Alexieffe, 1963, Fr.)
The Octopus Bone (Yasuji Murata, 1927, Jap.)
Odor-able Kitty (Chuck Jones, 1945, US)
Old Czech Legends (Jiri Trnka, 1957, Cz.)
Old Glory (Chuck Jones, 1939, US)
The Old Man and the Sea (Alexander Petrov, 1999, Rus.)
The Old Mill (Walt Disney, 1937, US)
Oliver and Company (George Scribner, 1988, US)
On the Waterfront (Elia Kazan, 1954, US)
Once Upon a Time (Jan Lenica and Walerian Borowczyk, 1957, Pol.)
One Froggy Evening (Chuck Jones, 1956, US)
One Glass Too Many (Bretislav Pojar, 1953, Cz.)
101 Dalmatians (Walt Disney, Wolfgang Reitherman, Hamilton Luske and Clyde Geronomi, 1961, US)
One Million Years BC (Don Chaffey, 1966, UK)
1001 Arabian Nights (Jack Kinney, 1959, US)
Orpheus (Caroline Leaf, 1971, US)
Our Friend the Atom (Walt Disney, 1957, US)
The Owl Who Married A Goose (Caroline Leaf, 1974, Can.)
Pacific 231 (Mikhail Tsekhanovsky, 1930, USSR)
Pas de Deux (Norman McLaren, 1967, Can.)
The Passengers of the Great Bear (Paul Grimault, 1941, Fr.)
Passing Days (Nedeljko Dragic, 1969, Yug.)
Peace on Earth (Hugh Harman, 1939, US)
Peace, Love and Understanding (Mike Judge, 1993, US)
Pencil Story (Moira Marguin, 1995, Fr.)
Perfect Moon (Satoshi Kon, 1997, Jap.)
The Perimeters of Light and Sound and Their Possible Synchronisation (Mary Ellen Bute, 1932, US)
Permutations (John Whitney, 1968, US)
Peter and the Wolf (Caroline Leaf, 1968, Can.)
Peter Pan (Clyde Geronimi, Hamilton Luske and Wilfred Jackson, 1953, US)
*Picnic on the Grass (*Priit Pärn, 1988, Est.)
Pictures from a Gallery (Lillian Schwartz, 1976, US)
The Pied Piper (Walt Disney, 1933, US)
Pink Konkommer (Marv Newland, 1990, Can.)
The Pink Phink (Isadore 'Friz' Freleng, 1964, US)
Pinocchio (Walt Disney, Ben Sharpsteen and Hamilton Luske, 1940, US)
Plane Crazy (Walt Disney and Ub Iwerks, 1928, US)
Plane Daffy (Frank Tashlin, 1944, US)
Playful Pluto (Walt Disney and Burt Gillett, 1934, US)
The Playful Robot (Dusan Vukotic, 1956, Yug.)
Pleasures of War (Ruth Lingford, 1999, UK)
Pluto's Judgement Day (Walt Disney and David Hand, 1935, US)
Plymptoons (Bill Plympton, 1990, US)
Pond Life (Candy Guard, 1993, UK)
Poor Cinderella (Max Fleischer, 1934, US)
Popeye the Sailor meets Sindbad the Sailor (Max Fleischer, 1936, US)
Porco Rosso (Hayao Miyazaki, 1992, Jap.)

Porky's Duck Hunt (Fred 'Tex' Avery, 1937, US)
Porky's Hare Hunt (Ben Hardaway, 1938, US)
Post (Mikhail Tsekhanovsky, 1929, USSR)
Prince of Egypt (Brenda Chapman, Steven Hickner and Simon Wells, 1998, US)
Princess Honomoke (Hayao Miyazaki, 1999, Jap.)
Princess Iron Fist (Wan Brothers, 1940, China)
Puss Gets the Boot (William Hanna and Joseph Barbera, 1940, US)
Puss in Boots (Walt Disney, 1922, US)
Quasi at the Quakadero (Sally Cruickshank, 1975, US)
Quiet Please (William Hanna and Joseph Barbera, 1945, US)
Raga (Jordan Belson, 1959, US)
Raggedy Ann and Andy (Richard Williams, 1976, UK)
Raging Bull (Martin Scorcese, 1980, US)
Ragtime Bear (John Hubley, 1949, US)
Rainbow Dance (Len Lye, 1936, UK)
Red Hot Riding Hood (Fred 'Tex' Avery, 1943, US)
Red Riding Hood (Dudley Buxton and Anson Dyer, 1922, UK)
Remains to Be Seen (Jane Aaron, 1983, US)
Rembrandt (Oscar Grillo, 1992, UK)
The Rescuers Down Under (Hendel Butoy and Mike Gabriel, 1990, US)
Revenge of the Trees (Guido Manuli, 1993, It.)
The Revolving Table (Paul Grimault, 1988, Fr.)
Rumba (Norman McLaren, 1939, US)
Rhythm in Light (Mary Ellen Bute, 1934, US)
Rhythmus 21 (Hans Richter, 1921, Ger)
The River is Red With Blood (Wan Brothers, 1938, China)
Roujin Z (Katsuhiro Otamo, 1991, Jap.)
Ruff and Reddy (William Hanna and Joseph Barbera, 1957, US)
Rumba (Norman McLaren, 1939, US)
Saludos Amigos (Walt Disney, 1942, US)
The Sandcastle (Co Hoedeman, 1977, Neth.)
The Sandman (Paul Berry, 1990, UK)
Satiemania (Zdenko Gasparovic, 1978, Yug.)
Screenplay (Barry Purves, 1992, UK)
Screwball Squirrel (Fred 'Tex' Avery, 1944, US)
The Sculptor's Nightmare (William Bitzer, 1908, US)
Seance (Jordan Belson, 1959, US)
Second Class Mail (Alison Snowden and David Fine, 1984, UK)
The Secret of NIMH (Don Bluth, 1982, US)
The 7th Voyage of Sinbad (Nathan Juran, 1958, US)
Sex and Violence (Bill Plympton, 1998, US)
The She-Devil (Kihachiro Kawamoto, 1972, Jap.)
Shrek (Andrew Adamson and Vicky Jenson, 2001, US)
The Silly Goose (Hans Fischerkoesen, 1945, Ger.)
Sinbad: Beyond the Vale of Mists (Evan Ricks, 2000, Ind.)
Sing Beast, Sing (Marv Newland, 1980, Can.)
Sinkin' in the Bathtub (Hugh Harman and Rudolph Ising, 1930, US)
Sinking of the Lusitania (Winsor McCay, 1918, US)
Sioux Me (Ben Hardaway and Carl Dalton, 1939, US)
Sirène (Raoul Servais, 1978, Bel.)
Sisyphus (Marcell Jankovics, 1974, Hun.)
Skeleton Dance (Walt Disney and Ub Iwerks, 1929, US)
Slapstick (Clive Whalley, 1994, UK)
Slow Bob in the Lower Dimensions (Henry Selick, 1990, US)
Snipe Clam Grapple (Hu Jinqing, 1984, Ch.)
Snow White and the Seven Dwarfs (Walt Disney and David Hand, 1937, US)
The Snowman (Hans Fischerkoesen, 1943, Ger.)
Solid Serenade (William Hanna and Joseph Barbera, 1946, US)
Some Exercises for an Independent Life (Priit Pärn, 1980, Est.)
Song of Spring Flowers (Arnaldo Ginna, 1910, It.)
Song of the Prairie (Jiri Trnka, 1953, Cz.)
Song of the South (Walt Disney, 1946, US)

Songs of the Anti-Japanese War (Wan Brothers, 1938, Ch.)
South of the Border (Walt Disney, 1942, US)
Soviet Toys (Ivanov and Buskin, 1924, USSR)
Space Jam (Joe Pytka, 1997, US)
Spawn (Todd McFarlane, 1999, US)
Spook Sport (Norman McLaren and Mary Ellen Bute, 1940, US)
Springer and the SS (Jim Trnka, 1946, Cz.)
Star Trek: The Wrath of Khan (Nicholas Meyer, 1982, US)
Star Wars (George Lucas, 1977, US)
Stars and Stripes (Norman McLaren, 1939, US)
Steamboat Willie (Walt Disney and Ub Iwerks, 1928, US)
Steelman No 28 (TCJ, 1965, Jap.)
Stop That Car! (Bruno Bozzetto, 1993, It.)
The Story of a Mosquito (Winsor McCay, 1912, US)
The Story of the Flag (Anson Dyer, 1927, UK)
Street of Crocodiles (Quay Brothers, 1986, UK)
The Street (Caroline Leaf, 1976, Can.)
Stressed (Karen Kelly, 1994, UK)
Stuart Little (Rob Minkoff, 1999, US)
Study of the Effects of Four Colours (Arnaldo Ginna, 1910, It.)
Superman (Max Fleischer, 1941, US)
Superman (Richard Donner, 1978, US)
Synchromie (Norman McLaren, 1971, Can.)
Synchromy No 2 (Mary Ellen Bute, 1935, US)
Taking a Line for a Walk (Lesley Keen, 1995, UK)
Tale of Tales (Yuri Norstein, 1979, USSR)
The Tale of the Fox (Ladislaw Starewich, 1930, Fr.)
A Tale of Two Kitties (Bob Clampett, 1942, US)
Tango (Zbigniew Rybczynski, 1982, Pol.)
The Tango (Gianluigi Toccafondo, 1991, It.)
The Tantalising Fly (Max Fleischer, 1919, US)
Tarantella (Mary Ellen Bute, 1939, US)
Tarzan (Chris Buck and Doug Liman, 1999, US)
The Tell-Tale Heart (Ted Parmelee, 1953, US)
The Terminator (James Cameron, 1984, US)
Terminator 2: Judgement Day (James Cameron, 1991, US)
Texas Tom (William Hanna and Joseph Barbera, 1950, US)
Thank You Mask Man (John Magnuson and Jeff Hale, 1968, US)
That's Nothing (Phil Mulloy, 1990, UK)
Théâtre de M.et Mme Kabal (Walerian Borowcyck, 1967, Fr.)
There Lives a Man Called Kosyavin (Andrei Khrzhanovsky, 1966, USSR)
The Thief and the Cobbler (Richard Williams, 1995, US)
Three Blind Mice (George Dunning, 1945, Can.)
The Three Cabelleros (Walt Disney, 1944, US)
Three Little Pigs (Dudley Buxton and Anson Dyer, 1922, UK)
Three Little Pigs (Walt Disney, 1933, US)
3 Misses (Paul Driessen, 1998, Hol.)
Three Orphan Kittens (Walt Disney, 1935, US)
Through the Glass Ceiling (Jane Bradshaw, Milena Dragic, Janis Goodman, Stephanie Munro and Terry Wragg, 1995, UK)
Tin Toy (John Lasseter, 1989, US)
Titan AE (Don Bluth, 2000, US)
Toot, Whistle, Plunk, and Boom (Walt Disney, Ward Kimball and Charles Nicholls, 1953, US)
The Top (Jimmy Murakami, 1965, UK)
The Tortoise and the Hare (Walt Disney and Wilfred Jackson, 1935, US)
Tout Rien (Frédéric Back, 1979, Can.)
Toy Story (John Lasseter, 1995, US)
Toy Story 2 (John Lasseter, 2000, US)
Train Collision (Segundo de Chomòn, 1905, Sp.)
Transmutation (Jordan Belson, 1947, US)
The Triangle (Priit Pärn, 1981, Est.)
Trikfilm III (George Griffin, 1973, US)

A Trip to the Moon (Georges Méliès, 1902, Fr.)
Tron (Steven Lisberger, 1982, US)
Tweetie Pie (Isadore 'Friz' Freleng, 1947, US)
25 Ways to Give Up Smoking (Bill Plympton, 1989, US)
Two Faces (Alison De Vere, 1969, UK)
The Two Sisters (Caroline Leaf, 1990, Can.)
Ubu (Geoff Dunbar, 1978, UK)
Un Point, C'est Tout (Claude Rocher, 1986, Fr.)
Uproar in Heaven (Wan Brothers, 1965, Ch.)
Use Instructions (Guido Manuli, 1989, It.)
V for Victory (Norman McLaren, 1941, Can.)
The Valley of Gwangi (James O'Connelly, 1968, US)
Variations (John and James Whitney, 1941, US)
Vertigo (Alfred Hitchcock, 1958)
The Victor (Phil Austen and Derek Hayes, 1985, UK)
Victory Through Air Power (Walt Disney and David Hand, 1943, US)
A Visit to the Spiritualist (J. Stuart Blackton, 1897, US)
Walking With Dinosaurs (Tim Haines, 1999, UK)
The War and the Dream of Momi (Giovanni Pastrone, 1916, It.)
The Weather (George Barber, 1995, UK)
Weather-Beaten Melody (Hans Fischerkoesen, 1942, Ger)
Western Daze (George Pal, 1941, US)
Wet Paint (Jules Engel, 1977, US)
The Whale (Noboro Ofuji, 1927, Jap.)
What on Earth (Les Drew, 1975, Can.)
What's Opera, Doc? (Chuck Jones, 1957, US)
When the Wind Blows (Jimmy Murakami, 1986, UK)
Who Framed Roger Rabbit (Robert Zemeckis, 1988, US)
Who Killed Cock Robin? (Walt Disney and David Hand, 1935, US)
Why Man Creates (Saul Bass, 1968, US)
The Wife of Bath's Tale (Joanna Quinn, 1998, UK)
The Wild Hare (Fred 'Tex' Avery, 1940, US)
The Wild Planet (René Laloux, 1973, Fr.)
Wilfred (Peter Kershaw, 2000, UK)
William Blake (Sheila Graber, 1978, UK)
Winsor McCay Makes His Cartoons Move (Winsor McCay, 1911, US)
Winter Trees (Sarah Downes, 1993, UK)
The Wise Little Hen (Walt Disney, 1934, US)
The Wizard of Oz (Victor Fleming, 1939, US)
The World of Power and Women (Kenzo Masaoka, 1932, Jap.)
The Wrong Trousers (Nick Park, 1994, UK)
Yantra (James Whitney, 1955, US)
The Yellow Submarine (George Dunning, 1968, UK)
You – The Living Machine (Walt Disney, 1958, US)
You Ought to Be in Pictures (Isadore 'Friz' Freleng, 1940, US)
The Young Grey Hen (Norman McLaren, 1947, Can.)
Your Face (Bill Plympton, 1987, US)

BIBLIOGRAPHY

The bibliography lists works cited in the text and is also designed to point to useful further reading. The annotated list of 'essential reading' highlights works considered to be of particular imporatance to contemporary understandings of animation, although many valuable contributions are also to be found under 'secondary reading'.

ESSENTIAL READING

Barrier, M. (1999) *Hollywood Cartoons: American Animation in the Golden Age.* New York and Oxford: Oxford University Press.
An extraordinarily detailed and potentially definitive account of the Golden Era of animation in the United States.

Bendazzi, G. (1994) *Cartoons: One Hundred Years of Cartoon Animation.* London: John Libbey.
Essentially 'the bible' for any initial enquiry and defining perspective of animation historically and globally.

Klein, N. (1993) *7 Minutes.* London: Verso.
An insightful account of the aesthetic and cultural inflections of Golden Era animation, relevant to many aspects of contemporary work.

Pilling, J. (ed.) (1992) *Women and Animation: A Compendium.* London: British Film Institute.
An important contribution to the study of animation, including articles and profiles about neglected but profoundly significant women artists in the field, compiled by one of the leading figures in the exhibition and study of the form.

Russett, R. and C. Starr (1976) *Experimental Animation.* New York: Da Capo.
Still one of the most important studies in the field, which concentrates on what some have argued is the 'purest' form of animation: that made by experimental, avant-garde and individual artists specialising in the abstract, non-linear and non-objective form.

Wells, P. (1998) *Understanding Animation.* London and New York: Routledge.
A small piece of 'trumpet-blowing' but not a bad introduction to the form in relation to approaches, narrative, comedy, representation and audiences. This book is, in effect, its companion piece.

RECOMMENDED READING

Adams, T. R. (1991) *Tom and Jerry.* New York: Crescent Books.

Adamson, J. (1975) *Tex Avery: King of Cartoons.* New York: Da Capo.

Allan, R. (1999) *Walt Disney and Europe.* London: John Libbey.

Allen, R. C. and D. Gomery (1985) *Film History: Theory and Practice.* New York: McGraw Hill.

Barthes, R. (1984) 'The Death of the Author', in *Image, Music, Text.* London: Flamingo, 149–9

Beck, J. and W. Friedwald (1989) *Looney Tunes and Merrie Melodies.* New York: Henry Holt and Co.

Bell, E., L. Haas and L. Sells (eds) (1995) *From Mouse to Mermaid: The Politics of Film, Gender and Culture*. Bloomington and Indianapolis: Indiana University Press.
Blair, P. (1994) *Cartoon Animation*. Laguna Hills, California: Walter Foster Publishing.
Brion, P. (1990) *Tom and Jerry*. New York: Crown.
Bryman, A. (1995) *Disney and his Worlds*. London and New York: Routledge.
Byrne, E. and M. McQuillan (1999) *Deconstructing Disney*. London and Sterling: Pluto Press.
Cabarga, L. (1988) *The Fleischer Story*. New York: Da Capo.
Canemaker, J. (1987) *Winsor McCay: His Life and Art*. New York: Abbeville Press.
____(ed.) (1989) *Storytelling in Animation*. Los Angeles: American Film Institute.
____(1996) *Felix: The Twisted Tale of the World's Most Famous Cat*. New York: Da Capo.
Caughie, J. (ed.) (1993) *Theories of Authorship*. London and New York: Routledge.
Cholodenko, A. (ed.) (1991) *The Illusion of Life*. Sydney: Power Publishers.
Cotta Vaz, M. (2000) 'Engendered Species', *Cinefex*, 82, July, 68–93.
Crafton, D. (1993) *Before Mickey: The Animated Film 1898–1928*. Chicago and London: University of Chicago Press.
Davies, P. and P. Wells (eds) (2001) *Cinema and Society in America*. Manchester: Manchester University Press.
Dyer, R. (1986) *Stars*. London: British Film Institute.
Edera, B. (1977) *Full Length Animated Feature Films*. London and New York: Focal Press.
Eliot, M. (1994) *Walt Disney: Hollywood's Dark Prince*. London: Andre Deutsch.
Frierson, M. (1994) *Clay Animation*. New York and Oxford: Twayne.
Furniss, M. (1998) *Art in Motion: Animation Aesthetics*. London and Montrouge: John Libbey.
Giroux, H. (1997) 'Are Disney Movies Good for Your Kids?', in S. Steinberg and J. Kincheloe (eds) *Kinderculture: The Corporate Construction of Childhood*. Boulder and Oxford: Westview Press, 53–69.
Gomery, D. (1994) 'Disney's Business History: A Reinterpretation', in E. Smoodin (ed.) *Disney Discourse*. London and New York: Routledge/American Film Institute, 71–86.
Grotjahn, M. (1957) *Beyond Laughter: Humor and the Subconscious*. New York: McGraw Hill.
Halas, J. (1987) *Masters of Animation*. London: BBC Books.
Hollis, R. and B. Sibley (1988) *The Disney Studio Story*. New York: Crown.
Hollister, P. (1940) 'Genius At Work: Walt Disney', *Atlantic Monthly*, 166, 6, 689–701.
Hooks, E, (2000) *Acting for Animators*. Portsmouth, NH: Heinemann.
Jones, C. (1990) *Chuck Amuck*. London: Simon & Schuster.
Kagan, N. (1982) *American Skeptic*. Ann Arbor: Pieran Press.
Kaminsky, S. M. (1985) *American Film Genres*. Chicago: Nelson Hall.
Kilborn, R. (1986) *Multi-Media Melting Pot*. London: Comedia.
Langer, M. (1995) 'Why the Atom is Our Friend: Disney, General Dynamics and the USS Nautilus', in M. Pointon (ed.) *Art History [Cartoon: Caricature: Animation]*, 18, 1.
Langer, S. (1973) *Feeling and Form*. London: Routledge and Kegan Paul.
Laybourne, K. (1979) *The Animation Book*. New York: Crown.
Leyda, J. (ed.) (1988) *Eisenstein on Disney*. London: Methuen.
Lindvall, T. and M. Melton (1994) 'Toward a Postmodern Animated Discourse: Bakhtin, Intertextuality and the Cartoon Carnival', *Animation Journal*, 3, 1, 44–63.
Maltin, L. (1987) *Of Mice and Magic*. New York: NAL.
Martin, K. (2000) 'Poultry in Motion', *Cinefex*, 82, July, 118–31.
McCloud, S. (1993) *Understanding Comics: The Invisible Art*. New York: HarperCollins.
McKee, R. (1999) *Story*. London: Methuen.
Merritt, K. (1989) 'The Little Girl/Little Mother Transformation: The American Evolution of Snow White and the Seven Dwarfs', in J. Canemaker (ed.) *Storytelling in Animation*. Los Angeles: American Film Institute, 105–23.
Mosely, L. (1986) *The Real Walt Disney*. London: Grafton.
Noake, R. (1988) *Animation*. London and Sydney: MacDonald Orbis.
Orr, J. (1993) *Cinema and Modernity*. Cambridge: Polity Press.
Peary, D. and G. Peary (eds) (1980) *The American Animated Cartoon*. New York: Dutton.
Pilling, J. (ed.) (1984) *That's Not All Folks: A Primer in Cartoonal Knowledge*. London: British Film Institute.
____(1997) (ed.) *A Reader in Animation Studies*. London: John Libbey.
Pointon, M. (ed.) (1995) *Art History [Cartoon: Caricature: Animation]*, 18, 1.
Polan, D. (1985) 'A Brechtian Cinema? Towards a Politics of Self-Reflexive Film', in B. Nicholls (ed.) *Movies and Methods, Vol. II*. Los Angeles: University of California Press, 140–52.
Pummell, S. (1996) 'Will the Monster Eat the Film?', in M. O'Pray (ed.) *British Avant Garde Film*. London: John Libbey/University of Luton, 299–315.

Quiquemelle, M. C. (1991) 'The Wan Brothers and Sixty Years of Animated Film in China', in C. Berry (ed.) *Perspectives on Chinese Cinema*. London: British Flm Institute, 175–87.
Roche, J. (1999) *Comedy Writing*. London and Chicago: Hodder.
Sandler, K. (1998) 'Gendered Evasion: Bugs Bunny in Drag', in K. Sandler (ed.) *Reading the Rabbit: Explorations in Warner Bros. Animation*. New Brunswick: Rutgers University Press, 154–72.
Sarup, M. (1993) *An Introduction Guide to Post-Structuralism and Post-Modernism*. London and New York: Harvester Wheatsheaf.
Schickel, R. (1986) *The Disney Version*. London: Michael Joseph.
Schneider, S. (1988) *That's All Folks: The Art of Warner Bros. Animation*. New York: Henry Holt.
Smith, D. R. (1987) 'New Dimensions: Beginnings of the Disney Multiplane Camera', in C. Solomon (ed.) *The Art of the Animated Image*. Los Angeles: American Film Institute, 37–49.
Smoodin, E. (ed.) (1994) *Disney Discourse*. London and New York: Routledge/American Film Insitute.
Solomon, C. (ed.) (1987) *The Art of the Animated Image*. Los Angeles: American Film Institute.
Taylor, R. (1996) *The Encyclopaedia of Animation Techniques*. Oxford: Focal Press.
Thomas, F. (1976) *Walt Disney: A Biography*. London: W. H. Allen.
Thompson, R. (1984) 'Duck Amuck', in J. Pilling (ed.) *That's Not All Folks: A Primer in Cartoonal Knowledge*. London: British Film Institute, 11–13.
Wasko, J. (2001) *Understanding Disney*. Cambridge and Malden: Polity Press.
Watts, S. (1997) *The Magic Kingdom: Walt Disney and the American Way of Life*. New York: Houghton Mifflin.
Wells, P. (ed.) (1997) *Art and Animation*. London: Academy Group/John Wiley.
____(1999) 'Thou Art Translated: Animated Adaptations', in D. Cartmell and I. Whelehan (eds) *Adaptations*. London and New York: Routledge, 48–57.
____(2000) *The Horror Genre: From Beelzebub to Blair Witch*. London: Wallflower Press.
____(2001a) 'Art of the Impossible', in G. Andrew (ed.) *Film: The Critics' Choice*. Lewes: Ivy Press.
____(2001b) *Animation and America*. Edinburgh: Edinburgh University Press.
____(2001c) 'Roughnecks: Reality, Recombancy, and Radical Aesthetics', *Point*, 11, Spring/Summer, 48–55.
____(2002) 'Where the Mild Things Are', *Sight and Sound*, 12, 2, 26–7.
____(fortchcoming) *British Animation: An Industry of Innovation*. London: British Film Institute.
Wootton, A. 'Animation and Dynamation: Ray Harryhausen interviewed', in J. Boorman and W. Donohue (eds) *Projections 5*. London and Boston: Faber & Faber.
Yoe, C. and J. Morra-Yoe (1991) *The Art of Mickey Mouse*. New York: Hyperion.
Zipes, J. (1995) 'Breaking the Disney Spell', in E. Bell, L. Haas and L. Sells (eds) *From Mouse to Mermaid: The Politics of Film, Gender and Culture*. Bloomington and Indianapolis: Indiana University Press, 21–43.